How Probate Works

A Guide for Executors, Heirs, and Families

Disclaimer

This book is not intended to be a substitute for personalized advice from an attorney. Nothing contained within this text should be construed as legal advice. The publisher and author make no representation or warranty as to this book's adequacy or appropriateness for any purpose. Similarly, no representation or warranty is made as to the accuracy of the material in this book.

Purchasing this book does not create any client relationship or other advisory, fiduciary, or professional services relationship with the publisher or with the author. *You alone* bear the *sole* responsibility for assessing the merits and risks associated with any tax or financial decisions you make.

How Probate Works

A Guide for Executors, Heirs, and Families

By Anthony S. Park

Copyright © 2019 Anthony S. Park
All rights reserved. No part of this publication may be reproduced or distributed without the express permission of the author.
ISBN: 9781795484244
www.anthonyspark.com

Dedication

To family,
who along with time and health,
are so much more important than money

Thank you for your feedback

Hearing directly from you, the reader, is the best way for me to make these books as useful as possible.

Please share how this book has helped you, or any suggestions for how I can make it better. You can email me at probate@anthonyspark.com or call me at 212-401-2990.

Thanks in advance for your feedback.

Best,
Anthony S. Park

TABLE OF CONTENTS

Introduction 1
　Who is this book for?
　Why a probate guide is so important
　The goal of this book
　A brief outline

Chapter 1.
Probate Definitions and Basics 5
　What does probate mean?
　What is a probated will?
　Why probate a will?
　When probate is needed
　Is it necessary to go through probate without a will?
　How long does probate take?
　How much does probate cost?
　Key takeaways

Chapter 2.
How to Obtain Letters Testamentary 21
　Who starts the probate process?
　Determining where to probate an estate
　What are letters testamentary?
　Getting letters testamentary
　Key takeaways

Chapter 3.
How to Settle an Estate **33**
   How to collect an estate
   How to find estate assets
   How to value an estate
   How to sell estate assets
   Opening an estate account
   How are estate debts paid?
   Paying expenses, debts, and heirs
   How to file final tax returns
   Key takeaways

Chapter 4.
How to Close an Estate **51**
   How to do an estate accounting
   Who inherits the estate?
   How to distribute estate assets
   Key takeaways

Chapter 5.
The Executor Guide **63**
   Why being an executor is difficult
   How to choose the executor (and whether to accept, if you're the named executor)
   When the executor or administrator declines to serve or drops out
   Making the executor job manageable
   Common complaints from heirs (and how to deal with them)
   Key takeaways

Chapter 6.
What to Expect When You're an Heir 81
  Why being an heir is hard
  When heirs collide
  Common complaints about executors
  Key takeaways

Chapter 7.
Special Situations in Probate 97
  Contested wills
  Minor or disabled heirs
  International estates
  Kinship hearings
  The estate is never probated
  Key takeaways

Next Steps 106

About the Author...107

Index..108

INTRODUCTION

Family, death, and money. Probate throws all this at you, and more. It can feel overwhelming. But it doesn't have to.

WHO IS THIS BOOK FOR?

This book is for executors, heirs, or anyone else involved in a probate estate. Whether you're in charge of the estate as executor, or waiting for your inheritance as an heir, this book is intended to help you understand and navigate the probate process from start to finish.

This is **not** a do-it-yourself, step-by-step guide to every granular task in the entire probate process. Rather, this guide is meant to give you a high-level overview of the process as a whole.

WHY A PROBATE GUIDE IS SO IMPORTANT

Getting probate right isn't just about making sure everyone gets their rightful inheritance (although that's certainly important, too).

It's also about making sure you exit the process with your family relationships intact, and hopefully even stronger than before.

THE GOAL OF THIS BOOK

My goal is for this guide to be an easy-to-understand overview of the entire probate process, so that you won't feel in the dark for any of the many steps.

I assume your goal is to gain just enough knowledge to work with your attorney intelligently (because you probably have better things to do than read hundreds of pages or dozens of blogs trying to become a probate or estate expert).

After you read this guide, I recommend that you work with an experienced attorney or professional executor to get personalized advice.

So why bother reading the guide at all?

1. You may realize that the process isn't as complicated as you feared;

2. You will learn from illustrative examples based on real-world cases; and

3. When you start to work with your attorney or executor, you'll have a basic understanding of probate ahead of time.

A BRIEF OUTLINE

In Chapter 1, **Probate Definitions and Basics**, we answer the basics, such as: what is probate, when is it needed, how long does it take, and how much does it cost?

INTRODUCTION

Chapters 2 through 4 go into more detail, digging into **How to Obtain Letters Testamentary**, **How to Settle an Estate**, and **How to Close an Estate**.

In Chapter 5, **The Executor Guide**, we explore the process from the executor's perspective, such as why being an executor is difficult, whether to accept if you're named executor, and common complaints from heirs.

In Chapter 6 we flip to the heir perspective and discuss **What to Expect When You're an Heir**, including why inheriting can be hard, when heirs collide, and common complaints about executors.

Finally, in Chapter 7 we review **Special Situations in Probate**, such as will contests, minor or disabled heirs, international estates, kinship hearings, and unprobated estates.

Let's get started.

CHAPTER 1.

PROBATE DEFINITIONS AND BASICS

Many people are familiar with the word "probate," but relatively few can accurately define it or the underlying processes it describes. This is unfortunate because death is an unavoidable fact of life. At some point, your parent, spouse, or sibling will die, and the process of settling the estate will begin.

Knowing what to expect—and potential pitfalls to avoid—will help you get through settling the estate more easily, with your sanity and family relationships (hopefully) intact.

WHAT DOES PROBATE MEAN?

Probate is technically defined as the legal process of authenticating the deceased's last will and testament, assuming he left one.

But people more commonly understand probate as the entire process of settling someone's financial affairs after death. Under that definition, there are three distinct stages of probate:

1. Certifying the will (if there is one) as valid through a court process, and appointing an executor or administrator;

2. Collecting and liquidating the deceased's assets, paying off debts, and filing the appropriate taxes, also known as "settling the estate"; and

3. Distributing the remaining assets to the beneficiaries and heirs in accordance with the will or state law.

WHAT IS A PROBATED WILL?

A probated will is simply a will that has been reviewed by a court and deemed valid. In other words, a judge has determined that the person who made the will was mentally competent and under no coercion to sign it, the document was properly witnessed, and it accurately reflects the wishes of the person who made it.

Once a will has been probated, its terms are binding and carry the force of law.

WHY PROBATE A WILL?

EXAMPLE: Imagine that your father died, naming you as executor and leaving everything to you and your brother equally in his will. Now imagine your brother is a greedy schemer and goes to the bank with your father's death certificate, hoping to withdraw all your dad's money and keep it for himself.

Probate protects both you and the financial institution from these types of unauthorized transactions. Once a will is probated, your lawyer helps you get letters testamentary (if there's a will) or letters of administration (if there isn't) that prove you're the court-appointed executor of the estate. You'll need these documents whenever you make any financial transactions with assets in the estate—and you can only get them after a will has been probated.

WHEN PROBATE IS NEEDED

Probate is a long, complex, and costly process, which is why some estate planners specialize in probate-avoidance strategies. But in most cases, an estate needs to be probated. In New York, for example, only an executor with letters testamentary or letters of administration can handle many of the tasks required to put a deceased's affairs in order—even something as simple as forwarding mail requires proper documentation.

Are there assets in his name only?

If you're wondering whether an estate needs probate at all, the simple answer is: if the deceased held any assets individually and in his own name only, the estate most likely needs to be probated, whether a will exists or not.

Probate is required for any assets owned solely in the deceased's name, including bank and brokerage accounts, real estate, tenants-in-common property, titled personal property such as cars or boats, and untitled personal property such as furniture, appliances, jewelry, and fine art.

Probate can be avoided, however, if the estate is small or contains only assets that pass by law to a named survivor or beneficiary.

For example, the deceased's share of property held in joint ownership with right of survivorship automatically transfers to the joint owner without probate. Assets owned by a revocable or living trust get the same treatment.

Other assets that don't need probate include accounts with named beneficiaries, such as life insurance policies and 401(k) or other retirement accounts.

It's important to note that naming beneficiaries or joint owners doesn't always work out the way the account holder intended, and is not a replacement for an actual estate plan.

EXAMPLE: Mr. Upton had three children and wanted them to share equally in his estate after his death. As it happened, he had brokerage accounts with roughly the same balance in each, so he named a different child as beneficiary on each of the three accounts.

Several years passed before Mr. Upton died, and as you'd imagine, the assets in each IRA performed differently. One held lots of Apple stock, one was loaded with Enron stock (ouch!), and one held tax-advantaged bond funds.

So, upon his death, Mr. Upton's "estate planning" through beneficiary designations was an epic fail in terms of carrying out his wishes to leave his money in equal shares to his children.

Examples of non-probate accounts

Many states permit naming a beneficiary for other financial accounts, such as brokerage and bank accounts. These are the most common "non-probatable" financial assets:

- **Payable on death (POD) accounts.** These are special bank accounts with named beneficiaries that can be set up for checking, savings, and money market accounts, as well as CDs and savings bonds. Once the beneficiary presents a death certificate, the money passes directly to him or her.
- **Transfer on death (TOD) accounts.** Brokerage accounts, stocks, and other securities can be held in designated TOD accounts. Most retirement accounts are TOD assets because they pass to the named beneficiary.
- **In trust for (ITF) accounts.** An ITF account holds assets in trust for another person. When the account owner dies, the money transfers automatically to the person named on the account.
- **Totten trusts.** Totten trusts are so named after a 1904 court case that found it was legal to open a bank account for another person who would have no right to the money until the account owner died. They are basically POD accounts.

It's important to note that designations in the above accounts supersede provisions in a will or trust. In other words, if Uncle Joe's will says the money in his brokerage account should be equally divided between you and your siblings, but the account itself names Cousin Sue as the beneficiary, Sue gets the cash.

Again, these "non-probatable" assets may not serve their intended purpose in conveying the account holder's wishes, especially since these designations override provisions in the will. Specifying your wishes in one central document, a will or trust, is a better way to guarantee they are carried out accurately.

EXAMPLE: Shortly after her divorce, Barbara fell head-over-heels for a man she was convinced she'd marry. She named him as beneficiary on several TOD savings accounts and CDs at her bank. A year later, they broke up, and Barbara completely forgot about the beneficiary designation, which happens all the time since beneficiary names usually aren't listed conspicuously on account statements.

When Barbara died many years later, those accounts — and the unknown and unexpected beneficiary — created a legal (and emotional) nightmare for Barbara's surviving husband.

Powers of attorney

This is a good time to mention power of attorney (POA) arrangements. Some people mistakenly believe that a POA allows the authorized individual to make decisions about a person's assets even after that person has died. This is not the case; powers of attorney become void upon death. At that point, decision-making rests with the duly appointed executor of the estate.

Small estates and summary probate

Some states allow "summary probate," which is a streamlined version of the probate process for small-value estates. "Small-value" can be misleading, however, because it applies only to the probatable portions of the assets.

EXAMPLE: If you died and left a home jointly owned with your spouse worth $600,000, a retirement account worth $500,000 naming your spouse as beneficiary, a POD bank account worth $200,000, and a smaller checking account worth $20,000, the total value of your estate would be over $1.3 million – however, only the small checking account worth $20,000 would be subject to probate. Thus, your estate would potentially qualify for summary probate.

The limits for summary probate vary by state. Some, like California ($150,000) and Nevada ($200,000), set the limit much higher than other states such as New York ($35,000) and North Carolina ($20,000). Only two states, Virginia and Delaware, don't have summary probate laws.

IS IT NECESSARY TO GO THROUGH PROBATE WITHOUT A WILL?

People either die testate (with a valid will) or intestate (without a valid will). The estate of someone who dies intestate is settled according to the state's laws of intestate succession, which determine who is eligible to inherit and the portion of the estate each heir will receive.

If the deceased person owned probatable assets, heirs need to go through the probate process to access them. The court will hear the petition for probate, appoint an administrator, and determine how assets will be distributed.

The same rules about assets and accounts that don't need to be probated apply whether the person dies with or without a will. In other words, you may be able to avoid probate without a will if the estate is small-value or all of the assets have named beneficiaries.

How long does probate take?

The short answer is: "A lot longer than you probably think."

Some estates are probated in as little as nine months, and others drag on for two to three *years*. Fifteen months is a realistic average for the entire probate process.

Here's a breakdown of what to expect:

1. Getting letters testamentary or letters of administration

During this stage, you need to collect signed and notarized documents from heirs and other interested parties, sometimes even disinherited family members (we'll go into more detail on why you need these documents in Chapter 2, How to Obtain Letters Testamentary). Although that doesn't sound too difficult, it can feel like herding cats. You may need to nudge (or occasionally nag) to get people to cooperate.

Once all of the documents are in order, everything is submitted to the court for processing, which typically takes between four and eight weeks. If everything is in order, and the court is operating efficiently, you should get your letters testamentary or letters of administration in about three months, start to finish.

But a lot of things can go wrong along the way and cause delays. Court delays are random and unpredictable. And in some cases, you may need a third-party hearing before the court can appoint an executor.

EXAMPLE: You're probating your uncle's will and there is no known address for one of the heirs. You take every possible step to find the missing relative, but he never turns up. The court requires extra steps to ensure every effort has been made to locate the heir, such as publishing a notice in local newspapers or assigning a government agency or third-party investigator to conduct a search and report to the court. These extra steps and court hearings could add months to the timeline.

2. Settling the estate

This part of the process is one of the reasons probate takes so long. First of all, there is a mandatory waiting period, which is seven months in New York, during which creditors can make claims against the estate. You can't close the estate until this waiting period has passed.

Some estates take much longer to settle, even as long as three years, although the average is closer to nine months. During the settlement stage, the executor collects and organizes all of the assets, pays any outstanding debts, and files the appropriate tax forms. If an estate tax return is necessary, you can automatically add 18 months to three years to the settlement phase for the closing letter to arrive from the tax authority.

Don't be surprised if bureaucratic incompetence causes delays. You'll be dealing with banks, insurance companies, and government agencies, so a little inefficiency is baked into the cake. Other common delays revolve around real estate or other illiquid assets.

EXAMPLE: Your grandfather owned several rental properties that you need to liquidate as the executor of his estate. You are able to sell and close on most of them in the first six months, but the tenants in the remaining property are uncooperative and refuse to leave. As a result, you have to initiate eviction proceedings, which adds a year to the settlement timeline.

3. Closing the estate

This stage typically lasts between one month and one year, with an average of three months. During this time, you're preparing closing documents and issuing checks to the heirs. Most people are motivated to get their paperwork signed, notarized, and returned so they can collect their share—but don't count on it. You may have to do a bit more nudging and nagging to get all of the documents in order.

At this stage, delays are usually caused by someone contesting the final accounting. That is, calling into question financial transactions made in the estate by the executor, such as whether the executor sold real property at a fair price, sold a stock quickly enough before it tanked, or overpaid for estate expenses.

These proceedings are unpredictable and can add months or even years to the closing timeline.

HOW MUCH DOES PROBATE COST?

Let's start by explaining the relationship between the probate lawyer and the estate. People mistakenly believe that the probate attorney represents the estate, when in fact, the attorney represents the executor or administrator. The executor represents the interests of the estate, and the attorney represents the interests of the executor. In other words, the attorney's obligation to the other heirs is very limited.

Probate fees are paid by the estate and are deducted before proceeds are distributed to heirs. Probate attorneys generally charge for their services in one of three ways: an hourly rate, a percentage of the estate, or a flat fee, in some cases.

EXAMPLE: Kathryn's mother's estate was fairly uncomplicated, with Kathryn and her sister being the only heirs. Kathryn hired a probate attorney for a flat fee of $10,000 to handle the entire process for her. The probate attorney gathered the estate assets of $300,000, then paid out debts and taxes of $40,000, leaving $260,000. After paying the probate attorney fee "off the top," $250,000 was left to divide equally between Kathryn and her sister.

State law generally provides maximum amounts an attorney can collect from an estate. Sometimes this is a percentage scale of the value of the estate, and sometimes it's based on a vague "reasonable fees" standard.

How much you will pay for a probate lawyer depends on exactly what you want him or her to do.

Getting letters

If you only need help probating the will and getting your letters testamentary (or letters of administration if there's no will), you can expect to pay a lower total fee, depending on potential complications.

What kind of complications? A poor quality or poorly drafted will, errors on the death certificate, an unusually high number of beneficiaries, or unexpected court appearances will add to the cost of getting your letters testamentary.

EXAMPLE: Jason's mom used a DIY kit to prepare her will 10 years ago when she lived in Chicago. Unfortunately, the will didn't include all of the required forms, such as affidavits from the witnesses. When Jason tried to probate her will in New York, where she died, he was unable to locate a witness to swear to the will's validity. His lawyer was ultimately able to find a witness and obtain a sworn statement, but it added several weeks and several thousand dollars in legal fees to the probate process.

Letters of administration may present an additional set of problems. In New York, as in most states, administrators appointed by the court in the absence of a will are required to get a probate bond that protects the heirs against a bad executor. If the court-appointed administrator has poor credit or other risks, he may not qualify for a bond.

In this case, a probate lawyer can step in, secure the bond, and take over on your behalf, but it will add to the cost of obtaining letters of administration.

Settling the estate

During the settlement phase, the probate attorney may help with setting up a bank account for the estate, liquidating assets, organizing and paying the estate's debts, and filing the appropriate tax returns.

Not everyone needs legal help during settlement. If you are the sole heir, or the estate is fairly straightforward, you may be able to manage most of these tasks on your own. On the other hand, you may still want to delegate these tasks because they can be time-consuming, especially if you live in another state.

If you do choose to hire a probate lawyer to help you settle the estate, be sure to discuss the different activities involved and ask for a customized quote if there are things you want to handle on your own.

EXAMPLE: Liza's father left a $3 million estate that included a beach home in St. Thomas. Liza felt comfortable organizing the domestic assets and paying most of the debt on her own, but she needed help disposing of the beach home and filing the appropriate taxes. Typical attorney fees for settling the estate would be as much as 2% to 3% of the estate's value (between $60,000 and $90,000 in this case). However, because Liza did much of the work herself, she was able to negotiate a flat fee of $25,000 for the specific legal services she needed.

Closing the estate

The final stage in the probate process is closing the estate. During this stage, you are preparing an accounting and disbursing funds to the heirs. Costs vary, but if the estate administration is messy—incomplete records, sloppy accounting, improper handling of tax returns—expect to pay more. Heirs (and creditors) will scrutinize the numbers.

In a straightforward closing, you may not need a probate attorney. If you are the executor and sole beneficiary, for example, or if the sole heirs are you as a surviving spouse and your children, closing the estate can be as simple as filling out receipt forms from the court clerk.

On the other hand, if there are many heirs, or there are strained relationships, the transparency provided by a probate attorney closing the estate may ward off potential problems.

EXAMPLE: Kelly had power of attorney over her ailing mother's finances for several years before her mother died. Kelly's younger sisters were resentful and often argued with her over the decisions she made on her mother's behalf. After her mother's death, emotions boiled over, and accusations of misconduct were leveled at Kelly. She chose to hire a probate attorney to handle the closing so that every detail was fully documented and reported, ensuring maximum transparency for her siblings.

It's tempting to cut corners on legal advice when you're closing the estate—you're so close to the finish line, and all that's left of your work is to file a few reports and send a few checks, right?

Wrong. The most important thing that happens during closing, from the executor's point of view, is that you are formally released from ANY future personal liability. Mess up here, and you're looking at a lifetime of potential lawsuits. If there's even a hint of risk or family discord, do yourself a favor, and hire a competent probate attorney to handle the closing for you.

KEY TAKEAWAYS

- Unless the estate is small and uncomplicated, you will need to go through probate, whether there is a valid will or not.
- Probate will take a lot longer than you expect: a year or more is typical.
- Attorney fees for probate are often negotiable—you can lower your costs by doing more of the legwork yourself.
- To eliminate your risk for future liability from disgruntled heirs, don't scrimp on good counsel when you close the estate.

CHAPTER 2.

HOW TO OBTAIN LETTERS TESTAMENTARY

You'd be forgiven for thinking that getting letters testamentary is a simple thing, maybe something your lawyer drafts in a day or two that you can pick up on your way home from work.

You'd also be mistaken. Unfortunately, like everything else in the probate process, getting letters testamentary is, well...a *process*. Let's walk through it, step by step.

We'll start at the very beginning, with who initiates the probate process and where probate usually occurs.

WHO STARTS THE PROBATE PROCESS?

In most cases, the executor (the person responsible for organizing the deceased's assets and debts) named in the will starts the probate process. If the deceased was ill or elderly, the will may have been discussed with a trusted family member or friend, and finding the document may be fairly easy.

Often, however, it's not that simple, especially in the case of an unexpected death. A little sleuthing may be in order. You may need to dig through file cabinets, comb the address book for an attorney's name, or even call your loved one's friends to find out if the deceased prepared a will.

If a will is located, it's the executor's duty to initiate probate. If there's no will, anyone with a material interest in the estate can petition the probate court. In fact, if the named executor is dead, disabled, or just not interested in taking on the job, someone else must step up to start the process.

Keep in mind, however, that there's a priority order when it comes to who initiates probate. If there is no will, or the executor is unable or unwilling to serve, the court looks to the spouse, child, grandchild, parent, sibling, niece or nephew, and so on through the family tree to serve as administrator and probate the estate.

Of course, a probate attorney can always step in as a professional executor if none of the other candidates is willing or eligible to settle the affairs of the estate.

EXAMPLE: When Julia's elderly spinster aunt passed away in her nursing home, naming Julia the executor of her will, Julia believed there were no assets to speak of in the estate. She wasn't particularly motivated to initiate the probate process, knowing it would require a lot of time and effort for little or no reward, so she simply put it on the back burner, hoping it would go away. Julia was quite surprised a few months later when she received notice that an estranged nephew initiated probate to collect a stash of savings bonds Julia didn't even realize her aunt had owned.

DETERMINING WHERE TO PROBATE AN ESTATE

Ideally, the deceased lived, died, and owned all her property in the same county, because then there's no question as to where to probate an estate.

It gets a little messier if the deceased owned real property in more than one county in the same state. In most cases, you'll open probate in the county in which the deceased lived, even if there's property in another county. But don't take that to the bank, because not all states handle multi-county assets in the same way.

It can get even more complicated if the deceased was the sole owner of property in multiple states. You may have to manage probate proceedings in both states, because real estate is always under the jurisdiction of the state it's located in, not the state the owner resides in.

EXAMPLE: When Ellen's father died, Ellen's mother leased the home she had shared with her husband in Delaware to a family friend and moved into a condo in Baltimore to be near Ellen and her family. After her mother's death, Ellen was discouraged to discover she had to manage two probate proceedings: a domiciliary probate in Baltimore, where her mother was living at the time of her death, and ancillary probate in Delaware, where her parents' home was located.

Some states do make allowances for ancillary probate. For example, depending on the state, you may be able to simply file a copy of the will and letters testamentary with the probate court in the other state in order to take control of the property there. Additionally, 23 states recognize special beneficiary deeds, which transfer on death without a probate process. This is especially useful if the deceased owns property in multiple states.

County of domicile determines where to probate a will for someone who died in a nursing home or other facility outside her home county. Generally, you would open probate in the county where the person lived prior to transfer to the facility, although some states and counties have different rules.

EXAMPLE: Eric's father was in the final stages of pancreatic cancer, so Eric and his wife moved him from his home in Westport, Connecticut, to their home in Queens to care for him until he died a few months later. Although his father actually passed away in Eric's home in Queens, Eric had to probate his father's estate in Fairfield County, Connecticut.

If the deceased lived and died overseas but had assets such as a bank account in the U.S., the probate process and where it happens may look a bit different. Ideally, you'll probate in New York, since most major U.S. banks have an office there and the state's probate laws are fairly straightforward compared to other states.

EXAMPLE: Adele and Niall were British citizens living in London, where Niall worked in the financial industry. Just prior to the EU referendum, when the pound was at a high, Niall transferred a large chunk of their savings to a U.S. bank. After Niall died, Adele had no idea how to recover that money. She hired a New York probate lawyer to establish Niall's U.S. estate in New York, file the federal transfer certificates, and release her cash.

Now that we know who starts probate and where it usually happens, let's discuss how to obtain letters testamentary. But first, what are they?

WHAT ARE LETTERS TESTAMENTARY?

We've already learned that the first part of the probate process involves naming the executor, settling the estate, and distributing the proceeds.

In the course of completing these tasks, the executor deals with banks, brokerages, insurance companies, government agencies, and any number of people and organizations requiring some form of proof that the person seeking access to the deceased's assets or privileged information actually has the legal authority to do so. Many executors think that if they are named in the will, they have all the authority they need. Unfortunately, that's not so.

That's where letters testamentary come in. These are court-certified documents authorizing you to act on behalf of the estate. Depending on where you live, and whether or not you were named as the executor in the deceased's will or appointed by the court in the absence of a valid will, these documents may be called different things. Whether they're called letters testamentary, letters of administration, letters of personal representative, or any other name, their purpose is to prove that you are legally allowed to conduct business for the estate.

EXAMPLE: Shortly after Seth's father died, he needed cash quickly to cover some urgent expenses in his father's estate. As the executor named in the will, he assumed it would be no problem to go to the bank with his father's will and the death certificate and withdraw the necessary funds. He was frustrated when the branch manager told him that those original documents weren't enough. After all, there was no proof that the will Seth brought in was the most recent, or even valid under the law. He explained that Seth would need letters testamentary to access his father's account.

GETTING LETTERS TESTAMENTARY

Please note that the process below describes steps that are *typically* involved in obtaining letters testamentary (or letters of administration if there's no valid will). *The exact process in your county or state may be very different.*

The probate process can vary from county to county, let alone state to state, so you should consult an attorney in the county where probate will be opened, or contact the appropriate probate court for local requirements.

Collect your documents

For both letters testamentary and letters of administration, you'll need an original copy of the death certificate and a family tree with contact information for all surviving family members.

From there, the document requirements slightly differ.

Letters testamentary
In addition to the death certificate, you'll need the original will.

Most states, including New York, require all next of kin and those in line to inherit to be notified that probate has been initiated, even if provisions in the will specifically exclude a particular family member. To verify that everyone has been notified, you'll need a signed court waiver form from each family member. If someone refuses to cooperate or doesn't respond, you'll need to have a court hearing.

Once you've assembled the package of documents, you'll submit it, along with a filing fee based on the size of the estate, to the court for processing.

Letters of administration

You'll need a copy of the deceased's funeral bill showing that it has been paid in full, along with the death certificate.

You'll also need to prepare a list of assets and liabilities. This should include everything from real estate, bank accounts, insurance policies, and personal property to mortgage loans, credit cards, and unpaid taxes. It's OK if you don't have *exact* figures, but you do need to give a reasonable estimate. The court won't accept documents with a question mark or "TBD" in place of actual numbers.

You'll also need to submit a filing fee to the court along with your document package.

Keep in mind that during the letters phase of probate, there may be issues that crop up, triggering court hearings and other delays. These will be discussed in greater detail in Chapter 7, Special Situations in Probate.

Establish your eligibility as executor

The baseline qualifications for a *named executor* are actually pretty loose. At a minimum, you must be a U.S. citizen, at least 18 years of age, and mentally competent to qualify in most states. Some states bar felons from serving as executors, even if they're named in the will. Others have no such restrictions (Oregon and New Jersey come to mind—in fact, in New Jersey, the named executor can actually be incarcerated and carry out his duties!). In states where discretion is allowed, courts tend to err in favor of the deceased's wishes in appointing an executor.

In the absence of a will, however, this discretion doesn't apply. Courts adhere to fairly strict standards of trustworthiness when granting letters of administration.

Some states, including New York, also require the executor or administrator to be a resident of the state in which the estate is probated. Others require a local co-executor if the executor lives out of state. Most courts require an out-of-state executor to obtain a probate bond.

What is a probate bond?

A probate bond, also known as an executor or administrator bond, is a type of insurance that protects the estate against illegal actions or fraud committed by the executor or administrator. Bonds are underwritten by private bonding companies, and premiums are based on your credit score and the size of the estate.

Courts in some states require all executors to obtain a bond, while others only require them in specific situations, such as when there is a disagreement among the heirs, or when the executor is a convicted felon. (Side note: In states where felons *are* permitted to serve, they are almost always disqualified by the bond requirement.)

Most courts require all administrators to obtain a bond. It's important to note, however, that judges have the ultimate authority over whether or not to require a bond in a probate case.

EXAMPLE: Ginger's colleague Julian, a fellow partner in her New York accounting firm, named her the executor of his estate in his will. After Julian's death, Ginger was surprised and disappointed to learn that his children were unhappy with his choice – they argued strenuously that the eldest son should act as executor. Although Ginger was well qualified to do the job and was entrusted with the task in Julian's will, the probate judge ordered her to obtain an executor bond before granting letters testamentary.

What happens if I can't get a bond?

This happens a lot more often than you might expect. Bond companies can have pretty strict underwriting standards.

If it happens to you, you're not without options. You can hire an attorney to serve as the professional executor to get around the requirement.

Some states also allow the heirs to jointly agree to waive the bond requirement, especially if the executor is also an heir.

The testator, or maker of the will, can also waive the bond requirement in the will, although some states allow the court to overrule a bond waiver if there are reasonable grounds to require one.

EXAMPLE: When 18-year-old Liam and 20-year-old Noah unexpectedly lost their mother, Eileen, they were shocked to discover she had not left a will. Both boys were still in school, and neither had a job or any significant credit history. Because Eileen's estate included a home that would have to be sold in order to settle her debts and enable the boys to finish their educations, the judge required an administrator bond. Given their slim financial profiles, neither boy could qualify for a bond. Fortunately, they were able to hire a probate attorney to serve as executor and manage the estate on their behalf.

Receive your letters

Once you've submitted all of your documents, obtained any required bond, and appeared for any required hearing, you're in a holding pattern while the court processes your paperwork. Most of the time, processing goes smoothly, and the clerk issues an order authorizing the letters testamentary or letters of administration.

It usually takes about a month or two after you submit your documents for the court to return them. The documents will name you as the fiduciary (either executor or administrator) and show the name of the deceased, date of death, and date of issue.

These aren't just run-of-the-mill documents plucked from a printer filled with standard Xerox copy paper. They are on printed on special paper with raised seals, official signatures, and maybe even a hologram, depending on where they're issued. Treat them with care—you'll need to present them to pretty much everyone you work with as you settle the estate.

Key takeaways

- You can't touch the deceased's estate without the appropriate court-certified letters testamentary or letters of administration.
- You don't get to choose where to probate an estate—state and county law determines where the probate process takes place.
- Even if a will names you as executor, you still have to meet certain qualifications and be approved by the court.
- It's very common for the judge to order a probate bond. If you can't get one, you may need an attorney to take over as a professional executor.
- Even though obtaining your letters should be a fairly straightforward process, don't be surprised if there are court hearings or other delays.

CHAPTER 3.

HOW TO SETTLE AN ESTATE

Now that's you're officially court-certified as the executor or administrator of an estate, the real work begins. Technically, the settlement phase involves identifying and collecting assets, paying the deceased's debts and any required taxes, and distributing the remaining assets to the heirs.

It sounds simple enough, but in reality, things can get a little dicey, especially if your loved one died suddenly or unexpectedly. Ideally, the deceased was organized enough to leave a will and a folder filled with estate planning documents and essential financial information.

But if things aren't exactly ideal? You have your work cut out for you. Here's the information you need to organize and settle an estate.

HOW TO COLLECT AN ESTATE

This is a process that involves so much more than just tracking down the deceased's assets, although that's a big part of it. In addition to inventorying and recording the estate's assets, you may need to get professional appraisals for some of them and ultimately liquidate them, depending on the deceased's wishes, the estate's debts, or state law.

You will need an estate account into which you can transfer all of the deceased's cash assets, deposit any funds acquired from selling assets, pay the estate's expenses, and disburse the funds.

What are considered estate assets?

Let's start by defining estate assets. Legally, the estate is everything the deceased owned in his name alone at the time of death. These assets must go through the probate court process in order to transfer ownership to the heirs. Examples of probate assets include real estate not held jointly with rights of survivorship, bank and brokerage accounts that are not payable or transferred on death (POD and TOD accounts), personal property, business interests in a corporation or partnership, and life insurance policies or other assets that name the estate as the beneficiary.

EXAMPLE: Mila and Jamie had lived together for 15 years in the home Jamie inherited many years ago. Most of Jamie's assets were in POD and TOD accounts naming Mila as beneficiary, and in his will, he left the home to Mila. After Jamie died, Mila assumed it was a simple matter of filling out some paperwork to put her name on the deed and collect the money in the accounts. She was partly correct: the POD and TOD accounts passed to her without probate. But the house, an estate asset whose deed was in Jamie's name only, had to go through probate before she could assume ownership.

Non-probate assets

Non-probate assets that may not be estate assets include life insurance and retirement accounts with named beneficiaries, certain types of bank and brokerage accounts that pay or transfer to a named beneficiary on death, jointly owned real property with rights of survivorship, and assets held in trust.

Beneficiary designations on non-probate assets like those mentioned above supersede provisions in the will.

EXAMPLE: Perry named his long-term girlfriend as the beneficiary on his life insurance, IRA account, and bank accounts. They broke up some years later, and Perry ultimately married and changed the beneficiary on his life insurance to his wife, June. Perry and June opened new joint bank accounts and used a kit to create new wills leaving all of their property to one another.

When Perry died, June contacted the brokerage where Perry's IRA was held so she could collect the money. She learned that Perry had forgotten to change the beneficiary on the account, but she was unfazed, since she had a valid will leaving all of his assets to her. Then the bank explained that the will didn't supersede the named beneficiary on the account, and the ex-girlfriend would receive the cash. Unfortunately, the IRA was a sizeable chunk of his estate, and June had no legal claim to the money.

Community property

If the deceased lived in a community property state (Arizona, California, Nevada, Texas, New Mexico, Washington, Wisconsin, Idaho, and Louisiana), the estate gets a little messy. By law, couples in these states own property equally. In other words, the deceased's estate is only 50% of the jointly owned and acquired property.

EXAMPLE: David's will left his estate in two equal parts: to his second wife, Helen, to whom he had been married for 20 years, and to his daughter, Gina, by his first wife. The estate included a $1.8 million home in Santa Barbara and about $1.5 million in cash accounts. When David died, Gina assumed she would inherit in the neighborhood of $1.75 million, or half the value of the estate. Due to California's community property laws, however, Gina ended up with just 25% of the estate (half of David's half). Helen got 75% (her 50% plus half of David's half).

How to Find Estate Assets

The goal of the first part of the settlement process is to collect, inventory, and record all of the estate's assets. You may need a few detective skills to help you on this document chase.

First, let's start with a list of documents you'll need to settle an estate:

- ❑ Bank, brokerage, IRA, and 401(k) statements, plus any beneficiary designations
- ❑ Life insurance policies (some older policies may require you to surrender the original documents with your claim)
- ❑ Real estate deeds, titles to cars, boats, etc.
- ❑ Appraisals for jewelry, artwork, or other unusual assets, especially insured pieces

- ❏ Business documents such as corporate bank accounts, corporate charters, and titles for business properties if the deceased owned interest in a closely held business
- ❏ Federal and state income tax returns for the past three years, including any gift tax returns
- ❏ Contact information for the deceased's CPA, financial advisor, and/or attorney

Wondering how to find estate assets? That's where the detective work comes in. If there are no estate planning documents, you'll need to look through personal papers, address books, checking account statements, and email contacts for evidence of a personal attorney, financial advisor, accountant, or insurance representative.

Reviewing past tax returns may also provide a few clues, as will the deceased's forwarded mail.

You should check with any banks where the deceased had accounts to see if she also had a safe deposit box.

If you're thinking there must be some sort of centralized database or website where you can find a list of the deceased's assets, you'd be wrong. Persistent legwork and digging is the only way to find them.

How to Value an Estate

Your next step is to assign a dollar amount to the assets and debts in the estate. The goal here is to get an accurate accounting of the estate's value for tax purposes and to ensure proceeds are fairly divided according to the deceased's wishes.

Some of this will be easy. Simply transfer the figures from the asset's statement at the time of death, or request an official date-of-death value from the bank or brokerage. Non-cash assets such as real estate, vehicles, jewelry, and valuable collectibles may require a professional appraisal, especially if there is more than one heir receiving a share of the proceeds or the estate is large enough to be taxed.

EXAMPLE: Mr. Connor was the executor of his business partner's estate, which included a family home, rental property, several pieces of heavy construction equipment he owned separately and leased to the business, and a fishing boat. Because Mr. Connor and his partner's three sons were to receive equal shares of the estate according to the will, they jointly decided to have the properties and equipment professionally appraised to determine exactly how much the estate was worth. Even though the heirs spent a couple thousand dollars on appraisal fees, they agreed it was worth the expense to make sure the estate was evenly divided and no one got "a better deal" than the others.

HOW TO SELL ESTATE ASSETS

Once the executor or administrator has court letters, he has the authority to handle all of the transactions necessary to liquidate the estate, including:

- Closing the deceased's bank accounts
- Directing the deceased's broker to sell off stocks and bonds and convert them to cash
- Hiring a real estate broker to list and sell real estate

- Listing or auctioning off personal property such as cars, jewelry, art, etc.
- Selling a small business
- Depositing all cash proceeds into the estate account

The process differs a bit depending on whether or not there's a valid will.

When there's a valid will

In most cases, the executor liquidates all of the estate's assets, except for special requests in the will. For example, if the will states, "I leave my home at 123 Central Avenue to my wife, Susan," the executor transfers the home. The same goes for other special requests such as a sports car or specific shares of stock (e.g., "I leave my Apple shares to my nephew Charles").

The only exception is when there isn't enough money to settle the estate's debts. In that case, the executor may need to liquidate special requests and pay out any remaining proceeds to the specified heir.

When there's no will

The administrator usually liquidates everything, except real estate, which is retitled to the heirs. Again, if there isn't enough to settle the estate's debts and expenses, the administrator may need to sell the real estate, too.

EXAMPLE: Mr. Rosen's estate included his Park Slope brownstone and $200,000 in bank accounts. Since the cash was adequate to cover the estate's expenses, and his daughters, the *heirs, wanted to keep the home, the administrator retitled the brownstone to the two women and sent them checks for their half of the remaining cash.*

State law generally favors liquidation over holding specific assets to preserve the actual value of the estate at the time of the deceased's death.

EXAMPLE: Wallace was the executor of Mrs. Denton's estate, which included several thousand shares in XYZ Corp worth $300,000 at the time she died. Wallace left the stock alone while he sorted out the estate's debts, a process that took several months. During that time, however, XYZ Corp filed for bankruptcy protection, wiping out 95% of the stock's value. He was now potentially liable to the heirs for the lost money.

The executor or administrator shouldn't be making any investment decisions, intentionally or not, as in Wallace's case. He is simply responsible for preserving the value of the estate at the time of death and passing it to the heirs.

OPENING AN ESTATE ACCOUNT

Once someone is dead, you're unable to use her existing bank accounts to conduct business. Don't even try to deposit funds or write checks from the deceased's account—it's illegal, which is why you need an estate account.

It's the executor's or administrator's job to open an estate account, which is simply a new account to hold the estate's cash and pay off debts and disbursements to heirs. All of the deceased's money from bank and brokerage accounts will be transferred into it, as well as proceeds from the liquidation of assets. Any income to the estate, such as rental income, are also parked there.

Only a court-certified executor or administrator can open an estate account. The bank will ask to see your letters before opening the account. You'll also need to apply for a new taxpayer ID from the IRS to open an estate account.

Non-estate assets

Life insurance and other assets with named, living beneficiaries are not part of the estate.

It's the executor's job to notify the named beneficiaries so that they can collect the proceeds of these accounts themselves. The executor must also report the value of the accounts to the court and the IRS for tax purposes, even though these are non-estate assets. Examples of non-estate assets include:

- Life insurance
- Annuities
- 401(k) accounts
- IRAs
- Pensions
- POD and TOD accounts
- Social Security and VA benefits
- Wages owed

Collecting non-estate assets is generally as simple as contacting the bank or insurance company and completing claim paperwork. You'll need to provide a copy of the death certificate.

Generally, non-estate assets can't be used to settle the estate's debts and expenses.

HOW ARE ESTATE DEBTS PAID?

Estate debts versus expenses

There's an important distinction between estate debts and expenses from the executor's point of view. Estate expenses are paid first before settling the estate's debts. The heirs get what's left after both of these are paid.

Estate debts are repayment obligations incurred while the deceased was alive, such as:

- Income taxes
- Medical bills
- Credit card bills
- Cell phone bills
- Loans against retirement accounts and other personal loans

Estate expenses are incurred after death and include:

- Funeral bills
- Executor, legal, and accounting fees
- Ongoing expenses during the probate process such as mortgages, utilities, property taxes, and condo fees

An estate claim is when a creditor takes the extra step of filing its debt with the probate court. Executors should give these debts a bit more attention over other types of debts because these creditors mean business.

PAYING EXPENSES, DEBTS, AND HEIRS

It is the executor's job to pay the estate's debts, but unfortunately, it's usually the heirs who get called by creditors. These callers should always be referred to the attorney for the estate; this usually puts an end to the calls.

Most states have a waiting period during which creditors can make estate claims. In New York, it's seven months. At the end of that time, the executor looks over all debts and claims, determines which are legitimate and, where possible, negotiates a settlement. Most creditors will waive penalties and interest during the probate process, and it never hurts to negotiate down principal balances.

As an executor, it's very important to follow the timeline and the order of payment (expenses, debts, heirs), or you could expose yourself to financial liability.

EXAMPLE: Diane was the executor of her neighbor, Mrs. Carlson's, estate. A naturally super-organized, Type A personality, Diane blew through getting her letters, opening an estate account, and transferring Mrs. Carlson's cash into it. She was surprised to see the account had over $50,000, more than enough, she assumed, to handle all of the estate expenses, with cash to spare.

As each bill came in, she quickly wrote a check to cover it — $9,000 to the funeral home, $10,000 to the hospital, $5,000 in miscellaneous medical bills, $10,000 to pay off assorted credit card bills, and even $99 for Mrs. Carlson's final cell phone bill. When she finished, there was still over $14,000 in the account, which would cover the attorney fees and still leave a small sum for Mrs. Carlson's nephew and sole heir.

A month later, she learned there was a $30,000 Medicare lien against the estate, making it insolvent. Diane tried everything to get the money back from the creditors she'd already paid, but of course it was a total waste of time. Ultimately, Diane herself, as the executor, had to pay from her own pocket the difference of what was owed to Medicare and the cash left in the estate after the lawyer's fees were paid, which came to almost $20,000.

HOW TO FILE FINAL TAX RETURNS

Taxes are probably the last thing you want to think about when someone dies, but this is one of the trickiest parts of settling an estate. You may have to deal with one or all of the following taxes: federal estate tax, state estate tax, inheritance tax, and income tax, both for the decedent and the estate. If you are tempted to scrimp on professional advice anywhere along the way, *this is probably not the place to do it.*

Federal estate taxes

This one seems to grab the most attention, but in reality, less than 1% of estates will need to file an IRS form 706, the United States Estate (and Generation-Skipping Transfer) Tax Return. In 2018, individuals can leave $5.6 million, and married couples $11.2 million, to their heirs without triggering an estate tax.

Keep in mind that non-probate assets are included when determining the value of the taxable estate, with limited exceptions in the case of certain types of trusts.

That's good news for 99% of you, but if you happen to fall in that 1%, don't even try to file your estate taxes without the help of a tax attorney. CPAs are great for certain types of returns, but this is an area of tax law best left to an experienced tax attorney.

The current estate tax rate is a whopping 40%, but if you are the inheriting spouse, you aren't liable for estate tax, regardless of how much is left to you. Of course, that doesn't relieve you of the obligation to file an estate tax return.

There are many other issues that can affect tax liability (step-up in basis, minority discounting, gift tax, to name a few), so it's always a good idea to speak with a tax attorney whenever estate tax is involved.

Estate taxes are generally due nine months after the date of death. A six-month extension is usually granted if requested before the due date—as long as you pay the estimated taxes with your request.

State estate tax

State estate taxes are based on the state where the deceased lived, not where the heirs live. Currently, Connecticut,

Delaware, Hawaii, Illinois, Maine, Maryland, Massachusetts, Minnesota, New York, Oregon, Rhode Island, Vermont, Washington, and the District of Columbia have estate taxes on the books.

Five other states have repealed theirs in the last one to five years, including Delaware, New Jersey, North Carolina, Ohio, and Tennessee, so if you're still trying to settle an old probate case in one of these states, you may have to deal with estate taxes.

The exemptions vary by state, with Massachusetts being the lowest at just $1 million. If the deceased lived in a state with estate taxes, consult a probate attorney or accountant to see if you have any exposure.

What's the difference between estate and inheritance tax?

The major difference is in who pays the tax. Estate taxes are paid out of the estate, off the top, before any money is distributed to heirs. Inheritance tax is paid by the beneficiary once the money has been received.

There is no federal inheritance tax. Only six states currently assess the tax, and it's different depending on where you live. If you happen to inherit money in Iowa, Kentucky, Maryland, Nebraska, New Jersey, or Pennsylvania, you should consult a tax attorney about your potential inheritance tax liability.

EXAMPLE: Javier's gross estate was valued at $7 million, which, after deductions and adjustments, resulted in a federal *and state estate tax liability of about $800,000. After paying the estate taxes and other estate debts and expenses, there remained about $4.5 million for his heirs, including $1 million to his lifelong friend, Tomas.*

Tomas's state levies a 15% inheritance tax on all heirs except spouses and children. As a non-relative, Tomas had to pay $150,000 in inheritance tax on the gift.

The final 1040

For tax purposes, the deceased and the estate are two separate taxable entities. The executor or administrator will need to file a final 1040 for the deceased by April 15th of the year following the date of death.

If the deceased didn't earn much money in the year he died, you may not be required to file a final 1040. The 2019 limit is about $20,000 for a married person who would have filed jointly, but the limit can and does change regularly. In practice, however, a final 1040 is almost always filed because it's the best way to let the IRS know the deceased has passed away.

The surviving spouse and the deceased can still file a joint tax return for the year the person died, unless the surviving spouse remarries. In that case, the deceased's filing status is married filing separate.

Most of the same rules apply to the final 1040 as any other 1040, but be prepared for unpleasant surprises. If the deceased didn't file for a year or two, or has outstanding tax liabilities, you'll probably find out about it when you're handling the final return. The IRS knows this is its last chance to collect, so it will scour the deceased's tax history for any missed payments and potential revenue. You should always consult a good CPA before you file any final income tax returns.

EXAMPLE: As part of settling her father's estate, Christine and her father's accountant submitted a final 1040 to the IRS along with the taxes owed. With that task out of the way, Christine turned to paying the other estate debts and expenses. A few weeks later, Christine was dismayed to receive a fat envelope from the IRS informing her that her father owed some $18,000 in back taxes and penalties from previous tax years.

The 1041 return

The executor needs to file a 1041 (the return form for estates and trusts) if the estate earns more than $600 in a year. The form is filed using the taxpayer ID you obtained to open the estate account.

The estate's income can be in the form of interest on investments, rent from property owned by the deceased, and even the salary the person earned before death but was collected by the estate.

The executor must choose the estate's tax year. Timing the return properly can have significant tax benefits (another good reason to consult a tax pro). Most estates will only file one 1041, but if probate drags on, you could file more than one.

You can wipe out estate income with deductions, which include:

- Income distributions to heirs
- Executor and other professional fees
- Administrative expenses for the estate, such as court costs and probate bond
- Miscellaneous expenses such as postage, safe deposit box rental, and travel expenses if they exceed 2% of the estate's adjusted gross income

EXAMPLE: Mrs. Buck owned a duplex; she lived in one side and rented the other. When she died in April, the first four months' rent on the duplex were reported on her final 1040. During the six months it took to probate her estate and transfer ownership of the duplex to her son, the rent payments went to Mrs. Buck's estate account and were reported on the estate's 1041.

Although you might be tempted to file the 1041 on your own, they can be tricky beasts, especially the schedule B deductions. Consult a tax professional to avoid making a mistake and potentially triggering an audit.

Speaking of audits

Yes, the deceased and the estate can both be audited. In fact, it happens about 10 times more frequently than for other types of tax returns. In 2018, for example, about 9% of estate tax returns were audited, compared to 0.5% for other types of returns.

It typically takes at least six months to get a closing statement from the IRS. If a return is audited, it will take a year or more to close.

Again, it's strongly recommended that you work with a tax lawyer or accountant for all estate tax issues—and be sure to get a closing statement or "no audit" letter from the IRS before wrapping up the settlement phase of the estate.

KEY TAKEAWAYS

- Beneficiary designations on POD and TOD accounts supersede the provisions of the will.
- The executor's role is to *preserve the estate's value*, not to make any investment decisions.
- The executor must open an estate checking account, and all estate dollars will flow through it.
- There is a legal order to paying the estate's debts and expenses. If the executor doesn't follow it, he may be financially liable for the consequences.
- The executor files several tax returns on behalf of the deceased and the estate. Always consult a tax attorney if estate tax is involved.

CHAPTER 4.

HOW TO CLOSE AN ESTATE

Everyone talks about closure after death, but if you're an executor or administrator, closure takes on a whole new meaning. During the estate closing process, the executor submits an estate accounting documenting every transaction made on behalf of the estate for all of the interested parties to review. If there are any disputes about the executor's management of the estate, the executor may be held personally and financially liable—he may pay for mistakes out of his own pocket.

Once the accounting is approved, the heirs receive the proceeds of the estate and release the executor from any future liability.

For the heirs, closing the estate is a chance to see each step taken by the executor. It's the time to tie up any loose ends and look forward to the finish line, which is finally coming into view.

Here's what to expect during the closing phase of probating an estate.

How to Do an Estate Accounting

Every state—and in some states, every court—has its own probate court forms for filing a final estate accounting. The estate accounting is simply an organized structure for reporting the money that flowed in and out of the estate account, plus a list of proposed final distributions to the heirs, once all of the expenses and debts have been paid. Everything needs a paper trail, from $30,000 realtor fees to $420 court filing fees. If you're an executor, you must have organized, detailed records and receipts.

EXAMPLE: George's probate assets were very simple, just a bank account with $100,000 in cash. His brother William, as the executor, was closing the estate and preparing to distribute proceeds to George's three children. His estate accounting looked something like this:

- *Collect $100,000 from George's account and transfer to the estate account*
- *Pay estate expenses (funeral, attorney, court costs, etc.) of $15,000*
- *Complete the tax returns and pay $5,000 in income tax*
- *Pay off George's American Express bill of $5,000*
- *Distribute the remaining $75,000 to the three children in equal $25,000 checks*

Is a lawyer necessary for an estate accounting?

There's no law that says the forms must be completed by a lawyer or a fiduciary accountant (the type of accountant specializing in estate matters), but it's a *really good idea.*
Courts require a lot of very detailed information, and it must be presented in the format specified by the court. It's not a matter of slapping a few numbers into an Excel spreadsheet, and there's no TurboTax Estate-Accounting kit that walks you through the process and files the forms for you with the push of a button. It's not something you can DIY and hope it turns out all right.

Many different people have a right to review, and potentially object to, the executor's accounting: heirs (of course), creditors, the IRS, and possibly even the Attorney General if there are charitable gifts involved. The attorney ensures not only that the right numbers make it onto the form, but also that everyone who needs a copy of the accounting is notified and has a chance to raise any disputes.

And considering what's on the line—your permanent release of all risk and liability for your actions executing the estate—it's not something you want to get wrong.

When is an estate accounting required?

Some states require a full accounting with every estate closing, others don't. In states where a full estate accounting isn't required, the executor has discretion to decide how much disclosure is needed, based on weighing the potential risks and costs. Her options for accounting range from high disclosure/high protection to low disclosure/low protection:

- **A full estate accounting submitted to and approved by the court** provides the highest level of protection for the executor, but it is also the costliest and most time-consuming option.

- **A full accounting reviewed and signed by all parties, but not reviewed by the court**, gives the executor the next-best level of protection.

- **A non-standard DIY accounting reviewed and signed by the parties, with no court review**, has a moderate level of protection for the executor.

- The executor can provide **no accounting and just collect signed receipts and releases**, but this offers very little protection. The lack of transparency exposes the executor to future liability on the undisclosed matters.

- The executor has no protection at all if he simply **sends the heirs their checks without any sort of accounting or release**. This is probably OK if the executor is also the sole heir, as in a wife closing her husband's estate, but it's a bad idea in the majority of situations. You'll be a walking target.

EXAMPLE: Ethan was the executor of his brother David's estate. David left all of his assets to his wife, Karen. Since Karen was the only heir, and Ethan shared a close and trusting relationship with her, he decided not to deal with the expense of an estate accounting and simply provided her with a spreadsheet of the transactions in the estate account when he sent her the check for the balance.

If you're the executor, you must decide what level of protection you need from the stakeholders in the estate going forward. Quite honestly, you only have options if the heirs appear to be harmonious and in agreement. If there are signs of trouble, such as pointed questions, disputes, or a refusal to sign the release, get the full estate accounting approved by the court.

There are definite drawbacks to obtaining the full court-approved accounting. You pay for the attorney and/or accountant's services to prepare the accounting, and the process adds several months to the estate-closing timeline. However, having the court-approved accounting is nearly ironclad protection against future lawsuits.

EXAMPLE: Maryellen was the executor for her sister Ann's estate, which was to be distributed equally to her four living children, Maryellen's nieces and nephews. The heirs were anxious to close the estate and collect their inheritance, which they felt was already much smaller than it should be due to expenses and a lower-than-expected sales price on Ann's home.

They asked Maryellen to skip a full accounting to save time and money, and she reluctantly agreed, on the condition that everyone sign a receipt and release. She felt Ann would have wanted her to cooperate with the children and had confidence that the release forms would protect her.

Four years later, Maryellen was shocked to find herself embroiled in a lawsuit. Her nieces and nephews sued her for selling their mother's house too cheaply. Ultimately, the court decided in her favor, but it cost her thousands in legal fees and countless hours of her time, not to mention the permanent damage done to her relationship with her sister's children.

Why would someone dispute the estate accounting?

In a perfect world, all executors would live up to their fiduciary responsibilities and all heirs and creditors would be pleased with the results.

In the real world, however, executors make mistakes, intentionally or not, and heirs get disgruntled—for good reason, or perhaps simply due to a mix-up in communications along the way. This often happens when there are people, money, and high emotions involved, or when heirs don't have access to all of the information the executor has.

EXAMPLE A: Mr. Tandon named his attorney, Mr. Reilly, the executor of his will. Mr. Tandon's estate included a mortgaged home in a declining neighborhood. As soon as he had his letters testamentary, Mr. Reilly contacted a broker to manage the sale of the home, but after three months, there had been few showings and no offers. He authorized the agent to drop the price from $320,000 to $310,000, given that the estate was paying $2,500 a month in mortgage, HOA fees, and utilities while the house was on the market.

Two months later, a qualified offer finally materialized at $295,000 – a full $25,000 below the original asking price.

Mr. Reilly directed the broker to close the sale at the lower price, believing it could be many months before another offer came through, during which time the estate would continue to pay the expenses. He felt it was time to cut losses and take a sure deal.

When the heirs saw the settlement figures on the house, they were angry that they had "lost" so much money on the sale of the home and refused to accept the accounting, asking the court to weigh in.

Heirs might also dispute an accounting if the executor failed to preserve the estate's value. Remember, it's not the executor's job to make investment decisions, no matter how well-intentioned.

EXAMPLE B: Andrew was the executor of his father's estate, which included $700,000 in index funds in a brokerage account. The market had been hot for the past several months, and financial analysts predicted it would continue to climb. Andrew decided to leave the money in the index funds until the last minute of the mandatory waiting period so that the shares could continue to grow in value while the probate process played out.

Unfortunately, funky economic indicators triggered a massive selloff, causing the funds to lose almost 15% in value in a matter of days. Andrew panicked and sold the shares for almost $100,000 less than their value at the time his father died.

Andrew's sister and co-heir was furious with his mismanagement of the brokerage account and asked the court to hold him accountable for the lost money.

Judges have complete authority to settle disputes. If a judge determined that Andrew mismanaged his father's estate by failing to preserve the value of the estate funds, she could deny Andrew's executor fees, or even make him cover his sister's loss out of his own pocket.

WHO INHERITS THE ESTATE?

Closing the estate means finally paying heirs their inheritance. If there's a valid will, the executor distributes the estate according to the instructions in the will. If there's not a valid will, the administrator distributes assets based on the state's intestate succession laws.

In some sticky situations, the court may punt inheritance issues to the closing stage rather than resolve them before naming an executor. This is how courts sometimes handle the question of whether a child born out of wedlock can inherit.

EXAMPLE: Mr. and Mrs. Brown's 29-year-old son Elijah died unexpectedly in a car accident and left no will. After his parents filed for letters of administration to settle his estate, they were notified that a motion had been filed alleging that Elijah had fathered an infant son out of wedlock, who would stand to inherit the entire estate under state intestacy laws.

The court issued the letters of administration to Mr. Brown and allowed him to begin the probate and settlement process, with the limitation that the issue of paternity must be resolved before any money could be distributed from Elijah's estate.

HOW TO DISTRIBUTE ESTATE ASSETS

Distributing estate assets is simply a matter of cutting checks for the heirs and closing the estate. But before the executor can cut any checks or transfer the title to Grandpa's 1962 Corvette to his grandson, the court must approve the estate accounting, or the executor must get signed receipt and release forms from the heirs and interested parties.

What's a receipt and release?

A receipt and release is actually exactly what it sounds like: it's an official, notarized court document stating that the person who signs the form approves of the executor's actions during his term, agrees with the proposed disbursements, and releases the executor of liability. In plain terms, the signer will not sue the executor at some later date.

If you're the executor, you probably already see how important these documents are for your future mental and financial well-being. You absolutely don't want to spend the rest of your life wondering if grumpy cousin Ned is going to wake up one day and sue you because you didn't treat him fairly in handling Grandpa's will.

Once the signed and notarized receipt and release documents are filed with the court, the executor cuts checks to the heirs. And just like that, the estate is closed. All that's left is closing out the estate account.

How to close the estate account

There's really nothing special about an estate account; it functions just like any other checking account. Once all of the checks have cleared, the account should be zeroed out and you can officially close it.

Be sure to get a letter from the bank stating the account is closed—you don't need a zombie account coming back to haunt you. Zombie accounts happen when the bank reopens a closed account without notifying the account holder. This is actually a standard practice among most major banks. Hidden in the fine print is a clause saying the bank may reopen your account without your knowledge if a credit or debit is posted to the account after you close it. An official closing letter protects you from transactions and fees occurring after that date.

EXAMPLE: During the probate process, which dragged on for over a year, Ted, the executor, decided to simplify his life and authorized automatic debits from the estate account for the utility bills on his brother's house. When the house finally sold, Ted closed the estate, zeroed out the estate account, and asked the bank to close it.

The new owners transferred all of the utilities into their name when the house closed but didn't realize there was a separate trash and recycling bill each quarter. The city debited the estate account for the bill, which triggered a zombie account reopening and a $35 overdraft fee. Because the overdraft wasn't resolved in five days, the bank charged another $15 fee...and another...and another.

By the time Ted saw a paper statement in the mail regarding an account he thought he'd closed, the account had a negative balance of almost $300. Ted quickly notified the new owners about the recycling bill, but he still had to cover the $300 in bank fees before he could close the zombie account.

KEY TAKEAWAYS

- Release from future liability is a major concern for the executor before closing the estate.
- If the court requires a formal estate accounting, you should definitely consult a probate attorney and/or fiduciary accountant. It's not a DIY project.
- If the court finds that the executor mismanaged the estate, it can hold the executor personally responsible for any financial loss.
- The executor should always get receipt and release forms from the heirs to reduce exposure to a future lawsuit.

CHAPTER 5.

THE EXECUTOR GUIDE

No matter what role you play in the estate, you'll want to read this guide. Executors get an eye-opening view of exactly what the job entails (and how to know if they're the right person for it), plus plenty of tips for navigating the process with their sanity intact.

Heirs learn what to do if a named executor declines the job and how a new executor is selected. And everyone involved in settling and closing the estate gets an insider's view into the life of the executor, what to expect along the way, and why it's actually a pretty thankless job. This guide may even help your family survive probate intact, without long-lasting grudges and relationship-ending squabbles.

WHY BEING AN EXECUTOR IS DIFFICULT

From an heir's point of view, the executor's job looks pretty cushy. The executor only has to close a few accounts, fill out a few forms, do a little math, and send out checks, right?

In reality, the executor's job is actually difficult and occasionally all-consuming. If you are confirmed as an estate executor, you'll have a number of challenges to look forward to.

Your tasks are non-delegable

Everything the executor has to do to settle and close an estate must be done by him personally. There's no power-of-attorney escape hatch to get you out of some of the mundane tasks—you'll be spending hours on hold with the insurance company, standing in line at the bank, and personally handling every statement, estate claim, and tax form.

You operate in a time warp

Every institution you will deal with while settling an estate is locked in 20th century mentality and technology. A few examples:

- With most non-probate court cases, you can e-file your paperwork with the court and submit digital documents. Not so when it comes to estates. You will have to physically go to court, meet with the clerk, and submit actual paper documents during the probate process.

- Need to open an estate account at the bank? You can't do it online like you do for personal accounts; it requires an in-person meeting at the branch. And if you're used to getting customer service through your app or web portal with your personal accounts, you'll be very disappointed by the process for estates. It's almost always done face-to-face or over the phone (after being transferred six times and spending 20 minutes on hold).

Everyone you deal with will have no idea what he's doing

Most customer support specialists aren't trained on estate issues. They may be competent handling most of the routine issues that come across their desks, but estates are not in the average customer service rep's wheelhouse.

Every encounter will escalate to a supervisor level before it can be resolved, and even then, the supervisor will need to check with the legal department or the accounting department before coming back with an (often wrong) answer.

Here's where a good lawyer is invaluable, because a lawyer knows which documents are necessary, which processes are required, and how to get the bank or insurance company to cooperate and move things along. If you need help dragging recalcitrant office workers along by the nose, an attorney is the right person for the job.

You are stuck in the middle

On one side, you're dealing with banks, insurance companies, government officials, and courts, all of which move at a glacial pace. On the other side are the heirs, creditors, and tax collectors who want immediate action and answers to their questions.

You, the executor, are squeezed from both sides, and there's not much you can do about it. And you will definitely get pushback if you try to rush the slow-moving official or slow down the impatient heir. You'll live in a state of frustration while the probate process plays out, so you might as well get used to it.

You're exposed to a *lot* of personal risk

If anything goes wrong while you're handling the affairs of the estate, you personally are financially liable. Screw up the order of payment, leaving an estate debt unpaid? You'll have to pay the debt out of your own pocket. Mismanage the sale of some stock? The judge might revoke your executor fees.

And it doesn't end there. Without a judicial accounting, there's no guarantee that a disgruntled heir won't pop up a year or two later and sue you for decisions you made settling the estate. Even if you're ultimately found not at fault, you'll be on the hook for legal fees to defend yourself. Accepting appointment as executor or administrator means exposing yourself to considerable personal risk and liability.

The pay is terrible

Yes, executors are paid and the rate is set by law, generally as a percent of the estate. But when you break down the countless hours spent administering the estate, you'd probably make more slinging lattes at Starbucks.

And don't be surprised if you're pressured by heirs to waive the fees, especially if you're a family member or friend. The heirs usually have no idea what goes on behind the scenes, so they feel like you're profiting off the death of a loved one.

How to Choose the Executor (and Whether to Accept, if You're the Named Executor)

Let's start by pointing out that you do *not* have to accept the role of executor, even if the deceased named you in her will. You can decline the job—that also applies to cases where there is no will and you are tapped to serve as administrator.

In fact, there are many good reasons why you might want to decline. Here's a checklist of requirements to keep in mind if you are thinking of accepting the job of executor (and for anyone you might ask to take on the role):

- ❏ **You live near the action.** This is actually a legal requirement in a lot of places, unless you have a local co-executor to handle all of the face-to-face encounters the job entails. Keep in mind, you're required to attend court hearings, manage liquidation of all local assets, and meet with the lawyers, accountants, and government entities where the deceased lived.

- ❏ **You have plenty of free time.** If you have a demanding career, are the primary caregiver for young children, or don't have a lot of flexibility in your schedule, this is not the role for you.

- ❏ **You have life experience in the non-digital era.** Don't laugh, but if you've only done business in today's technology-driven environment, you are going to be extremely frustrated handling an estate.

You can't tweet customer service for immediate answers, there's no app for your estate account, and yes, someone may actually want you to send her a *fax*.

❑ **You have gravitas**. A sense of confidence and personal authority goes a long way in managing the issues you'll face as an executor. You can get around this with a good attorney, but someone is going to have to get the bankers and insurance reps to cooperate and do what needs to be done. The best combination for untangling most estate issues is an authoritative executor and an experienced attorney.

❑ **You are risk-averse with a strong CYA mindset.** Disorganized free spirits aren't a good fit for the executor's job. Remember, you are personally liable for every decision you make related to the estate. You need to approach every situation with a healthy appreciation of the consequences of your decisions, and keep detailed records of every transaction you make.

If these statements don't describe you, or another person tapped for the job, do everyone a favor and find someone else.

WHEN THE EXECUTOR OR ADMINISTRATOR DECLINES TO SERVE OR DROPS OUT

There are many reasons someone may choose not to take on the job of executor or administrator. It could be illness, work issues, or general unsuitability for the task. When that happens, the court uses a priority order to choose a new executor.

Generally, if the named executor declines, or if there's no valid will, state law spells out the order of priority for next in line based on the will's named beneficiaries or the family tree.

EXAMPLE: When Mr. Stanton died, his will hadn't been updated in almost 30 years. This was unfortunate because the will named his wife as the executor of his estate. Mrs. Stanton, his widow, was 88 years old and suffered from dementia. Obviously, she was unable to serve.

The court first tapped Mr. Stanton's oldest son, Walter, for the job, but Walter's wife was newly diagnosed with colon cancer, and he declined to serve. Working through the list of relatives, the court ultimately appointed Walter's niece, Mr. Stanton's granddaughter, a part-time librarian living in the same city, who had both the time and the inclination to serve.

Hiring a professional executor

There are a lot of advantages to hiring an attorney to serve as a professional executor, especially when the estate is complex or there is a hint or history of family conflict.

For one thing, a professional executor is absolutely neutral. He represents the estate and the estate alone, meaning no one gets preferential treatment, and there is no *perception* of preferential treatment. In fact, the professional executor can serve as a referee or mediator when the inevitable family squabbles threaten to slow down the process.

And professional executors have experienced staff trained to efficiently deal with all of the mind-numbing parts of settling the estate, including any special circumstances. This is especially important if there are complex debts, illiquid assets, or tax planning issues at stake.

EXAMPLE: Frank was named executor of his brother Hal's estate in the will, but he was not looking forward to the job. Hal had recently acknowledged paternity of a 26-year-old son not born to his wife, a revelation that nearly destroyed his relationship with his wife and their two daughters. Of course, the young man stood to inherit after Hal's death, which Frank knew would be extremely painful for his nieces and their mother.

To make matters worse, about a year earlier, Hal had put up $150,000 in seed money for his son's tech startup in exchange for a stake in the company, which would now be an asset of the estate. It was a financial tangle Frank couldn't even begin to unwind.

Frank ultimately hired a professional executor to ensure his brother's estate would be settled neutrally.

Of course, a professional executor doesn't have to be an attorney. Banks can act as professional executors, but they rarely deal with estates valued at less than $5 million. CPAs and financial advisors have also been used in this role, but they are usually not the best choice, unless estate work is all they do.

Keep in mind, however, that professional executors are very selective in the cases they accept. The issue of personal liability is one no lawyer takes lightly, so you may have to interview a few lawyers before you find the right fit.

Using more than one executor

Some people think that sharing the executor job between two or more people would lighten the workload on each party, but that's really not how it works. Decisions made by committee are usually not the best decisions, and when decisions can't be agreed on, it starts a cascade of time-consuming consequences.

A co-executor may make sense if you are appointed the executor of an estate in another county or state where the court requires a co-executor who lives in the jurisdiction. Even then, the non-local executor may wish to decline to serve.

Also, two executors means the estate pays two sets of executor's fees, a situation the heirs would probably prefer to avoid.

MAKING THE EXECUTOR JOB MANAGEABLE

If you've agreed to take the executor job, there are a few things you can do to keep your sanity.

First, retain an experienced probate attorney to keep you on track and ward off potential problems along the way. Remember, you are personally financially responsible for any mistakes you make settling the estate: a lawyer's guidance is a pretty strong first line of defense against a potential lawsuit.

Second, find a CPA who is very experienced with deceased 1040 and 1041 returns. The CPA who files your own 1040s every year may not be the best choice. Estate accounting is much more than just collecting your statements and plugging numbers into a spreadsheet. In the event a formal accounting is required, all of your documents must be in order.

COMMON COMPLAINTS FROM HEIRS (AND HOW TO DEAL WITH THEM)

There *will* be complaints, and it's your job as the executor to deal with them early, even though it's tempting to brush them aside. If you don't, they may resurface when you're about to cross the finish line and close the estate. And that doesn't bode well for an executor. The heirs might not approve the accounting or refuse to sign a receipt and release. They may even bring a lawsuit against you—something you definitely want to avoid.

These are the issues that crop up most often, and a few strategies you can use to quell the complaints.

"You're keeping me in the dark"

As the executor, you have access to more information than the heirs. You talk to the lawyer, you know where you are with collecting assets, you obtained the appraisal on the house. On your end, things are going more or less according to plan and you know your next move.

The heirs, on the other hand, have no idea what's going on, what the process looks like, or how long each step is expected to take. Worse yet, they have bad memories. They forget what you told them on the phone last month.

You can avoid a lot of problems with a proactive approach. Right at the start, email (or snail mail, if the heirs prefer) an outline of the process with the most conservative time estimate for each step. It's better to underpromise and overdeliver than field multiple concerned calls from the heirs when your letters testamentary take four months instead of two.

Notify the heirs when each major milestone is complete. Tell them what's happening next and when to expect another update. And save all your emails and/or copies of letters on file in case an heir insists you're not communicating. (A good paper trail will help you in court, too, should you ever have to answer a complaint about your work.)

EXAMPLE: Celine was the executor of her father's estate, which was to be shared equally among her and her three brothers. Celine's youngest brother, Raymond, was going through a business bankruptcy – finances were tight and tensions were high between Raymond and his wife. They made it very clear they were anxious to get their share of the money as soon as possible.

Celine created a task list and timeline using Google Documents. She invited her brothers and sisters-in-law to view and leave comments on the document. She kept careful notes on it whenever she handled any issues related to the estate and was quick to respond to any comments and questions her family left on the document. The shared document kept everyone informed of the process.

Every month, she sent out a progress report telling the family what she'd accomplished, if there were any unusual issues, and what she'd be working on next.

Although the process didn't move quickly enough to please Raymond and his wife, they were at least able to see her steady progress, thus saving Celine countless anxious phone calls.

"You're playing favorites with Joe"

This is a very real problem for an executor. If the heirs perceive bias, real or imagined, the usual outcome is more lawyers, more fees, and a lot more time to close the estate. An heir who believes he is being treated unfairly gets very resentful, and tends to dig in his heels. You may need to go through a judicial accounting, which is very time-consuming and costly, when one otherwise wouldn't be needed.

It is in everyone's interest for you to avoid even a whiff of preferential treatment. If you are closer to one of the heirs, this can be challenging.

Make sure all heirs are included in any estate-related communications, and don't chat on the phone about estate business with the one you're close to. Keep everything in writing.

If you think your close relationship with the heir will make it hard for you not to show bias, you shouldn't be the executor. The family would do better with an impartial party or professional executor.

EXAMPLE: When Belle's brother Wallace died, she was concerned to discover she was the executor of the will. Wallace's oldest daughter, Elinor, had lived with Belle and her husband, Harvey, during her college years, and being childless themselves, they had grown extremely fond of the young woman and treated her like their own. They stayed close over the years, frequently taking vacations together. When Elinor's mother died, she even asked Belle to stand in as mother of the bride.

Belle knew it would be impossible to maintain the appearance of impartiality between Elinor and her three siblings. Their close relationship had often been remarked on within the family. Although she felt she was best equipped to manage her brother's affairs, Belle declined to serve as executor, and Elinor's younger brother was appointed instead.

"This is taking way too long"

You will hear this a *lot* as an executor, so you might as well get used to it. Heirs have no idea what's involved in settling an estate, and even when you walk them through the process, they will *still* say it's taking too long.

Get in front of these complaints by sending a *very* conservative timeline right off the bat. If your lawyer says something will take between two and four months to resolve, tell the heirs it will be four months.

Refer to item number one above and keep a solid paper trail.

(And when all else fails, send them a copy of this book so they better appreciate what a time-consuming job it is to be an executor.)

"When am I getting my money?"

Although inherited money is an unexpected windfall, it's not unusual for heirs to make or have plans for how to spend it. And sometimes, they get a little impatient waiting for the check to arrive.

Explain to the heirs that it is impossible to determine their share according to the will or state law until all expenses and debts have been paid. That requires waiting out the mandatory time period for creditors to file claims, at a minimum. From there, it may take time to liquidate assets and file taxes to get to the actual value of the estate.

And remember, there is a statutory order to disbursements and distributions from the estate. Expenses first, debts second, and heirs third. Ignore the proper order at your peril—the executor is personally liable for any mistakes and shortcomings in the estate.

EXAMPLE: Kip was the executor of his brother Karl's estate, which was to be divided evenly between Karl's two sons. Aside *from Karl's home, the largest asset was a brokerage account with a balance of nearly $300,000.*

Kip sent monthly updates to the boys as he moved through the settlement process. When Aiden, the oldest, saw that the brokerage account had been liquidated, he began calling Kip on a daily basis, arguing that he should be entitled to his share of the cash right away. Kip explained that he couldn't disburse any money until all of the expenses and debts were settled, but Aiden was relentless. He insisted that the sale of Karl's home would more than cover any expenses from the estate. Finally, Kip relented and cut Aiden a check for $150,000, his half of the brokerage account.

Kip had a nagging feeling he'd done something wrong, but he was relieved the following month when it looked as if he would close on the sale of Karl's house. Then the unthinkable happened – a title search turned up an unpaid lien against the house amounting to almost half the home's sale price.

In the final accounting, once the lien and other expenses were factored in, Aiden's total share came to just $110,000. Of course, he refused to return any of the money to Kip, who ultimately had to pay the shortfall out of his own pocket.

Be aware that there are some unsavory people operating inheritance funding services, which are about on par with payday loans and other loan shark-types. If an heir even hints at using such a service, you should adamantly counsel against it. These businesses front a chunk of the money to the heir in exchange for his total share once the estate is settled.

This is terrible both for the heir and for you as the executor. Not only will the heir forfeit as much as half his share in fees, but you'll have to deal with the funding agency hounding you for the heir's portion.

"You're taking money for this?"

Don't be shocked if you are pressured to waive your fee for managing the estate, especially if you are also inheriting something in the will. Most people have no idea how much work is involved in settling an estate. If they did, they'd understand what a bargain the typical executor fee really is.

Executor fees are usually set as a matter of state law. Even the state recognizes that you should get paid for this often thankless job.

You can't avoid a whisper campaign or pointed remarks, but you can take away the element of surprise. In your first communication with the heirs, mention that you will be compensated for your role and your expenses will show up in the final accounting. If your state sets the fees, let the heirs know in advance how the fees will be calculated.

And don't let the heirs convince you to treat this difficult, time-consuming work as a labor of love. Take the money—you earned it.

KEY TAKEAWAYS

- The executor's job is difficult and time-consuming; not everyone is cut out to do it. If you don't think you can, you have the option to decline.
- Executors are exposed to significant personal and financial liability. A good attorney and CPA are invaluable assets for protecting yourself.
- You can avoid a lot of potential difficulty with the heirs by providing regular, written updates and progress reports.

CHAPTER 6.

WHAT TO EXPECT WHEN YOU'RE AN HEIR

Although executors have the toughest job in the estate-settlement process, it isn't all sweetness and light for the heirs. In addition to mourning a loved one, you're on the sidelines of a lengthy and often frustrating sequence of events that's pretty much out of your control. Probate is painful even in the best of circumstances—and it can get downright dreadful if there are family disagreements or procedural roadblocks.

This chapter lays out what to expect when you're waiting on an inheritance, how to overcome common pitfalls, and what you can do if you feel like the process is breaking down.

WHY BEING AN HEIR IS HARD

Most families have a method for dealing with conflicts and disagreements. If you feel like your dad treated you unfairly in a particular situation, you can go to him, present your case, talk it out, and reach a resolution. If your brother is behaving badly toward you, you can argue it out with him and find a compromise. Everyone has a more or less equal voice in important family matters.

All of that changes, however, when a family member dies and you become an heir. The moment the probate process starts, family dynamics take a backseat to the law. And that can cause all kinds of unpleasant issues for heirs, such as:

The almost total lack of control

Once an executor or administrator has been duly appointed by the court, you have very limited rights over the disposition of your loved one's estate. Because the executor is exposed to significant personal risk, the court gives him broad leeway and (essentially) total control over managing the estate's affairs. You're a spectator, not an active participant.

You're still entitled to your opinions—but the executor isn't required to respect them. And if you're unhappy with any decisions the executor makes, there's basically nothing you can do until the closing stage, when it's time to approve the accounting.

It's a helpless feeling, especially if you were close to the deceased or more than superficially involved in her financial affairs.

EXAMPLE: Mr. Wynn was the executor of Rachel's mother's estate, and Rachel learned from one of Mr. Wynn's progress reports that he was hiring out some maintenance and repair work on her mother's home before listing it with a broker. Rachel's son Levi owned a small contracting business capable of doing the work. Levi had always been close with his grandmother, and Rachel felt sure her mother would have wanted Levi's company to get the job. So she showed the progress report to her son, and he wrote up an estimate and presented it to Mr. Wynn the next day.

When Mr. Wynn emailed Rachel and Levi that he had already chosen a contractor recommended by the broker, they were angry, and Levi demanded to know what the other company was charging for the work so he could match the bid. Mr. Wynn declined to discuss the issue further with them, and the other company completed the repairs.

Rachel was furious and brought the issue up at settlement, demanding to review each and every expense related to the repairs. She complained to the court that Mr. Wynn overpaid for the work, but the judge determined the expenses were reasonable and Mr. Wynn acted within his rights as executor in choosing the other contractor.

The feeling you're being kept in the dark...intentionally or not

The truth is that heirs have no legal right to weekly or monthly communications from the executor. From a strictly legal perspective, heirs are really only entitled to their rightful share when the estate closes.

In other words, once an executor is certified by the court, he is not legally obligated to take your phone calls or reply to your emails.

However, lack of communication is one of the most common complaints in probate court, and even though there isn't a *legal* requirement for regular, ongoing communications, most judges do expect the executors to share *some* information along the way. Given that it can take well over a year to settle an estate, it's unrealistic to expect the heirs to wait quietly without any information on the status of the process.

That said, heirs also need to moderate their expectations. As described in Chapter 5, The Executor Guide, most of the activities involved in settling an estate take a lot of time. Nothing moves quickly in probate, so it's not unreasonable to wait six months or more for a progress report. And courts give executors time to do their jobs—you'll be hard-pressed to find a judge to intervene with an uncommunicative executor before 6 to 12 months have elapsed.

Of course, you *do* have options short of petitioning the court. Retaining your own counsel to keep tabs on the executor can be a very efficient alternative.

EXAMPLE: Didi and her two sisters were at their wits' end with Ms. Keyser, the lawyer and family friend their father had chosen as executor of his estate. It had been six months since Ms. Keyser had been appointed by the court, and the sisters had not heard a word about their father's estate. They tried calling, emailing, and even sending a certified letter to Ms. Keyser's law firm, all to no avail.

Didi decided to hire an attorney to ask for a progress report on her and her sisters' behalf. Unsurprisingly, within three days of hearing from Didi's attorney, the sisters had a detailed letter from Ms. Keyser explaining everything she'd done with the estate and what to expect in the coming months.

Most people, lawyers included, tend to take notice when they receive communication on attorney letterhead. Ms. Keyser realized right away that the sisters were serious about monitoring her work on their father's estate, and was much more communicative during the rest of the settlement and closing process.

You become a target

Once an executor initiates probate on a deceased's estate, the names of the heirs are public record, available to anyone combing court documents. You might wonder why anyone would waste time digging through court records for information about heirs, but it's actually a common practice for all kinds of creditors and less-than-savory businesses.

Be on guard against the worst of the worst—inheritance funding services. These are businesses that approach impatient heirs and offer to advance money today against the amount the heir stands to inherit in the future. The rates are beyond usurious: it's not uncommon to get 50 cents on the dollar. Even if you're in a tight spot financially, it's best to avoid these scammers at all costs.

You may also be contacted by probate property buyers, which are usually tiny companies looking to pick up real estate on the cheap. They'll offer to pay cash today for Grandma's house, at rates well below market value, so you can avoid the time and expense of listing the home.

Refer these people to the executor. After all, you have no control over the sale of the home. It'll put an end to unwanted calls.

Don't be surprised if you're approached by creditors. Even though heirs are not liable for estate debts, these companies will contact you and appeal to your responsible nature. If they can get you to pay off a debt, it's a huge win for them. They get their money fast and don't have to wait out the probate process like everyone else.

Again, refer any creditor calls to the executor. You are not responsible for estate debts, and it's not your job to deal with collectors.

WHEN HEIRS COLLIDE

Even in tight-knit and generally agreeable families, a little friction during probate is pretty much inevitable. The probate process is unfamiliar and confusing: unexpected debts and expenses eat into the estate's value, and unintentional or perceived slights stir up tensions. Don't be surprised when conflicts occur.

And when they do occur, conflicts tend to fall into one of these categories:

It's all about the money

Heirs who are unhappy with the way their share of the estate is shaking out will usually preface their disagreement by saying, "It's not about the money." But in reality, it is pretty much *always* about the money. They might argue principles, fairness, or even "what Father would have wanted," but in the end, it's about what they think they're owed from the estate.

Which is not to say that these conflicts are always motivated by greed, or that they never have merit, only that in many cases, the intensity of the fight is in direct proportion to the size of the inheritance at stake.

If you're embroiled in a fight over money, be sure you have a good idea of the amount involved and what you're willing to spend to protect it—you don't want to get into a court battle where your legal fees exceed the amount of money you stand to inherit. It happens more often than you'd expect.

The assets are misvalued

Pretty much everyone can agree that spending $400 for an appraisal on the family home is worth the money. But when it comes to other assets, like cars, jewelry, or artwork, people aren't always willing to pay for an accurate valuation. That's unfortunate because misvalued assets can lead to unfair distributions in the final accounting—and that's a recipe for conflict.

In the case of cars, Kelly Blue Book offers fair market value. Accurate valuations for other personal property, such as boats, jewelry, or artwork, isn't quite so easy to find, but in most cases, it's worth paying reasonable fees to get fair market value. Transparency is the first step toward keeping everyone happy and avoiding hard feelings and/or legal challenges.

EXAMPLE: Carlton was the executor of his father's will, which specified that his estate be equally divided among his three children. Carlton planned to sell his father's home and auction off his personal property, splitting the proceeds between the three of them, but he knew his brother and sister wanted to keep a few of their father's things.

So Carlton invited his siblings to the house one afternoon to choose what they wanted before everything was sold. His brother, Neil, chose their father's collection of fine Swiss watches. His sister, Georgia, wanted the '65 Ford Mustang and an original Remington bronze. Carlton wanted a leather club chair and a large framed photo of his parents on their wedding day.

Carlton realized right away that these things were not of equal value, and he wanted to be as fair as possible in calculating each sibling's share of the estate. He decided to pay the appraiser at the auction house $300 to assign a value to the items each of the siblings kept from their father's property.

The appraiser valued the watches at $28,000, the car at $55,000, the sculpture at $40,000, and the club chair and wedding photo at $2,000.

The estate netted $153,000 from the auction, making $276,000 the total value of Carlton's father's personal property ($153,000 from the auction + $95,000 for the car and sculpture + $28,000 for the watches + $2,000 for the club chair and photo). Dividing the $276,000 value by three, each sibling would be entitled to $92,000 from personal property at settlement.

When Carlton completed the final accounting, each sibling's share of the personal property looked like this:

	Share of personal property owed	Value of items received		Amount due at closing
Carlton	$92,000	$2,000		$90,000
Neil	$92,000	$28,000		$64,000
Georgia	$92,000	$95,000		-$3,000

When Georgia got her check at closing, she was initially upset that it was significantly smaller than her brothers' checks. Carlton, however, was able to show her that she had, in fact, received an equal share of the estate due to the value of the items she kept from their father's personal property.

The shares are not equal

It is not unusual for a deceased's will to specify different dollar amounts or percentages to his heirs. Looking at the distributions in isolation can lead to hard feelings, especially if you're the one getting less than your siblings.

But it's important to look at the big picture—there are any number of reasons why a parent's will would specify a smaller or larger share to a child. Perhaps your father gave you $100,000 for a down payment on a house while he was alive, so he specified a cash gift of $100,000 to your sister in his will in addition to her equal share to balance things out.

Or perhaps you have a brother with a disability requiring full-time care, so your mother's will leaves a much larger share of her estate in trust to care for him.

The truth is, the deceased doesn't have to leave things equally to her heirs—it's completely within her right to dispose of her money any way she wishes, regardless of whether it seems fair to the people who inherit. The executor is legally obligated to divide the estate according to the wishes set forth in the will. You may not like it, but there's not much you can do about it.

EXAMPLE: When Claudia's mother was diagnosed with acute myeloid leukemia five years ago, Claudia and her husband moved her into their home to care for her. Treatment was unsuccessful and her mother declined rapidly. Claudia quit her job to provide care full-time over the remaining three years of her mother's life, even though it meant she and her husband would not be able to fully fund their retirement accounts or their children's college accounts.

After her mother died, Claudia was surprised and gratified to learn from the executor that her mother had made a special provision for her in her will. Claudia was to get the first $200,000 from the estate, with any remaining balance divided equally between Claudia and her sister, Josie. Of course, Josie wasn't thrilled about the unequal shares, but she recognized that Claudia had made great sacrifices to care for their mother, and it was within her mother's right to compensate Claudia for them.

The executor is not well suited to the task

It's impossible to put too much emphasis on choosing the right executor. If the named executor is a family member with obvious bias toward one heir over another, things will get contentious very quickly.

If the executor is someone without the time or temperament to do the job, the process will take much longer than it needs to, and delayed decisions may affect the overall value of the estate.

If the executor is also an heir, it's easy to spot evidence of self-interest, even where none exists.

If you have any concerns about the named executor, you should make your case to the court before letters testamentary are issued. Once the executor is certified by the court, you have very little recourse but to wait until the final accounting to air your grievances—and that may take years.

In many cases, a professional executor is a much better option than a family member or heir. The professional executor acts impartially on behalf of the estate and serves as a reasonable and detached referee when disagreements arise. You're also more likely to get regular progress reports and responses to your questions from a professional executor, and he'll act with authority to protect you from creditors and property scammers.

EXAMPLE: Debra was the business manager for the windshield repair franchise her father owned. She was also the named executor in his will. When her father died, Debra didn't see any conflict of interest with her settling his estate, but her two brothers definitely did.

The brothers knew that Debra's family relied on her income from the family business to pay their bills, and they worried that she would slow-roll selling off the business to settle the estate. They were also concerned that her role with the company put her in a position to manipulate financial information in a way that would benefit her at the expense of the other heirs.

The brothers ultimately persuaded Debra to decline the role of executor in favor of a professional executor. Although Debra was initially upset with her brothers, she came to recognize that the decision to use an independent executor saved their family relationships and avoided a lot of unnecessary drama.

COMMON COMPLAINTS ABOUT EXECUTORS (AND WHAT TO DO ABOUT THEM)

Every estate is different, and heirs can find any number of things to complain about during the probate process. That said, however, there are two complaints that crop up far more often than others:

"The executor is procrastinating"

This is a complaint that more often than not results from the heirs not truly understanding the settlement process. If you haven't familiarized yourself with the steps involved in collecting assets and settling an estate, you should do that first before taking any action.

It bears repeating that probate is a long and often unpredictable process, and it can easily take two years—or more—to complete.

In other words, your executor may not be procrastinating; he may simply be dealing with an unusual or complex situation in the estate.

Your first step should be contacting the executor to ask why there's a delay. Perhaps the letters testamentary were held up, for example, because an heir couldn't be located to sign a waiver, prompting a third-party investigation and court hearing.

Whatever the reason, your executor should be able to explain why the process has ground to a halt—and if the explanation seems fishy, you may want to get an attorney to prompt the executor to do his job.

And if all else fails, you can bring the situation before a judge to compel the executor to get moving.

EXAMPLE: Marlon's father passed away over a year ago, and he and his brothers were still waiting for the estate to close. In fact, they heard nothing from the executor for over seven months, until she notified the heirs that she was in the process of liquidating assets.

Marlon finally connected with the executor over the phone and asked her why nothing was happening with his father's estate. Mrs. Popham, his father's friend and executor, told him that things were at a standstill because there were tenants with a valid lease in his father's rental property and the broker had been unable to find a buyer for the home with tenants in residence.

That answer didn't satisfy Marlon, so he retained a lawyer to look into the executor's delay. The lawyer reviewed the situation and reassured Marlon that Mrs. Popham was in fact managing the situation correctly. Although the delay was still frustrating, Marlon had peace of mind about Mrs. Popham's work as executor – and Mrs. Popham, knowing that she had an attorney looking over her shoulder, was far more responsive to Marlon and his brothers going forward.

"The executor won't do her job"

Sometimes the named executor isn't motivated to start the probate process. It may be due to family matters—perhaps there's a new baby or a wedding to plan, for example—or time constraints from a demanding job. Whatever the reason, the executor hasn't taken any steps to get the ball rolling.

When this happens, your best option is to retain an attorney to determine who has standing to step in for the named executor. This may goad the named executor into action, and if not, you'll have a new executor in place who is willing and able to get the job done.

EXAMPLE: Mrs. Madera was in poor health the last years of her life, and she invited her granddaughter Jennifer to live rent-free in the other half of the duplex she owned in exchange for part-time caregiving and looking after the home. The arrangement worked well until Mrs. Madera passed away, leaving the duplex in equal shares to her four grandchildren and naming Jennifer the executor in her will.

Jennifer wasn't particularly motivated to start the probate process. She'd lived in the duplex for three years and loved the Brooklyn location – and she knew she'd never be able to afford rent on a similar place. So she decided to postpone opening probate on her grandmother's estate, offering one excuse after another to her cousins and co-heirs.

The other grandchildren were sympathetic to Jennifer's situation, and patient up to a point, but after two and a half years, Jennifer was still in the duplex. And to make matters worse, she'd rented out the other half and was pocketing the rent.

Their patience exhausted, the other heirs hired an attorney to petition the court to appoint a new, less conflicted executor and start the probate process.

KEY TAKEAWAYS

- Once an executor is duly appointed by the court, the heirs have few rights and very little control over the probate process.
- The executor has no legal obligation to share information with the heirs until the estate is closed. You can, however, ask the court to intervene if you've heard nothing after 6 to 12 months.
- An obstinate or uncommunicative executor generally responds pretty quickly to inquiries from an attorney. You may want to hire one to monitor the executor for your own peace of mind.
- If you have any qualms about the named executor, bring your concerns to the court *before* letters testamentary are issued. Otherwise, you're basically stuck until closing.

CHAPTER 7.

SPECIAL SITUATIONS IN PROBATE

With probate—as with just about any process dealing with legal issues—everything *seems* simple...until it isn't.

In other words, there's really no such thing as a "tiny" red flag. If you run into any of the following fairly common special situations, start looking for a good probate attorney.

CONTESTED WILLS

Whether you're the heir contesting the will, or the executor defending the will, the process is going to be messy.

What does it mean to contest a will?

In a nutshell, it means someone wants the court to throw out an existing will and call it invalid.

Not just anyone can contest a will; it must be an heir who benefits if the will is thrown out.

EXAMPLE: Jonas had been married just four months when he died, leaving his sizeable estate to his spouse in his will. His brothers and sisters, who long suspected the wife was simply a gold digger, were outraged that they were disinherited. However, if the will was declared invalid, Jonas's entire estate would still go to his wife under state intestacy laws, so the brothers and sisters lacked standing to contest the will.

Valid reasons to contest a will

Sorry to disappoint, but you cannot contest a will just because you think your share of the inheritance isn't "fair." To have a chance of success in court, one of the following three things must apply:

The will was improperly executed. Although requirements vary from state to state, most states require that the will contain certain legal phrases, be properly signed, and be witnessed by two "disinterested" parties.

EXAMPLE: Mr. Chatsworth prepared his will nearly 50 years ago, witnessed by two colleagues at his accounting firm. However, one witness was dead, the other could not be located at the time of Mr. Chatsworth's death. So, Mr. Chatsworth's estranged son, who had been disinherited in the will, contested it on the grounds that there was no proof (i.e., no witnesses) that the will was properly executed.

The decedent was incompetent. If you are contesting a will for competence, you will need medical records and other evidence to prove your loved one was not of sound mind when she signed her will. This can be quite difficult, because it often turns into an ugly and expensive battle of doctors' opinions. In addition, many courts recognize a "moment of clarity" when it comes to wills, further complicating the issue.

EXAMPLE: Shelly's mother had battled dementia for years before she died, and her periods of lucidity were fewer and farther between. Still, Shelly's petition to contest the will, which left most of her mother's estate to a charity for dogs, failed because her mother's doctor testified that she was still capable of lucid thought at the time of her death, that is, she had "moments of clarity" despite her illness.

The decedent was under undue influence. Of all the reasons to contest a will, this is the hardest one to prove. Undue influence requires proof that the decedent felt compelled to write his will in a certain way for fear of suffering serious reprisals.

EXAMPLE: Sophia quit her job to be the sole caretaker of her mother, who suffered from end-stage multiple sclerosis. In her will, Sophia's mother gave 75% of her estate to Sophia, leaving the remaining 25% to be shared between Sophia's sisters, Madeline and Helene. Helene contested her mother's will on the grounds that she rewrote it to favor Sophia out of fear that Sophia would stop caring for her unless she changed her will.

Imagine how hard it would be for Helene to prove her mother's fears, inner thoughts, and motivations. That's why these cases are uphill battles.

How to contest a will

Executors and administrators are generally required to notify all heirs (including folks who have been excluded or disinherited) that they are initiating probate. This is when you can contest the will.

If you plan to contest, you file a lawsuit and appear in court to state your objections. Know that contested-will litigation is a long, expensive, and unpredictable process—it can take years to settle a case.

And you don't just hire a lawyer to sue, then go on living your life uninterrupted. You must be prepared to give a deposition, which means that the opposing attorney interrogates you under oath with a court recorder. There is also discovery, which means you must share all of your documents with opposing counsel (and vice versa).

MINOR OR DISABLED HEIRS

Did you know that minor children can't technically "own" money? If a decedent names an heir under the age of 18, the child's money must be controlled by a court-appointed guardian until he reaches majority. (Estate planning note: this is why it's so important for parents to make wills, so that money goes into a trust and not directly to minor children.)

The same rule applies to a mentally disabled heir, and it still holds even if the minor or disabled child lives with a biological parent who is also an heir. The court will appoint a temporary guardian to represent the child's interest, which adds delays and expenses to the court probate process. As ridiculous as it seems, that's the current state of probate law.

EXAMPLE: Joaquim died without a will at age 31, leaving a wife and twin 3-year-old sons. Under state intestacy laws, his wife inherited half of the estate, with the other half split equally between his sons. Despite the fact that Joaquim's wife was also the biological mother of his sons, she still had to go through the court to be appointed guardian of her children's inheritance.

INTERNATIONAL ESTATES

Problems with international estates manifest in one of two ways: (1) A non-U.S. citizen dies abroad, but has assets in the U.S.; or (2) a U.S. resident passes away in the U.S., but all of her surviving heirs or relatives live abroad.

EXAMPLE 1: Neville was a British citizen who lived in London. He was mindful of currency exchange rates, so he kept a U.S. bank account to hold some of his savings in dollars, his only U.S. asset.

EXAMPLE 2: Lucy lived out her final years happily in lower Manhattan. When she passed, all of her relatives and next of kin were scattered across China, and none were U.S. citizens.

In the first example, the estate tax threshold for a non-U.S. citizen living abroad is just $60,000, which means that if Neville's U.S. bank account was above the threshold, his estate would owe estate tax.

Whether or not Neville's account was above the $60,000 threshold, however, his executor's letters testamentary alone wouldn't be enough to collect the U.S. accounts. U.S. banks and brokerages won't release the funds, even to a duly court-appointed executor, until the executor shows proof of U.S. tax clearance, either with an IRS clearance letter or Department of Treasury federal transfer certificates.

In the second example, the primary problem is finding a qualified executor to settle the estate. In most cases, an executor must be a U.S. citizen and reside in the country. If there is no one living in the U.S. who is qualified to serve, the best option is to hire a professional executor to probate and settle the estate.

Also, most probate documents must be notarized in the U.S. When heirs live overseas, that may involve a trip to the U.S. embassy and an appointment with the consul, which may take weeks or months to secure. In some countries, the fees are prohibitive, as much as $50 per page.

The notary issue can be avoided with an apostille, or "international notary." Only certain countries have this option, but if they do, there's no need to jump through hoops at the embassy to get a document notarized.

Unfortunately for Lucy's heirs, China does not have apostilles, and Lucy's heirs were scattered all across the Chinese countryside. For many heirs, it was extremely difficult to travel to the U.S. Consulate.

If you're dealing with international estate issues, an experienced probate attorney will help you navigate and plan for these issues.

Kinship Hearings

Whenever there's doubt about whether a person is *actually* related to the decedent—that is, actually an heir—the court will hold kinship hearings.

SPECIAL SITUATIONS IN PROBATE

Non-marital children are the most common reason for kinship hearings. In many states, children born out of wedlock bear the burden of proving the decedent is their biological father.

Unfortunately, the father's name on a birth certificate isn't enough to prove paternity in most states. In New York, for example, the non-marital child must show either DNA testing, a court order of paternity or child support, or a package of proof showing the father "openly and notoriously" acknowledged the child as his.

EXAMPLE: Nina was born through an affair between her mother and father, who was married to another woman. When her father died, she had to prove kinship in order to inherit her share of his estate. Although she didn't have a paternity test, she was able to show that her father had sent monthly checks to her mother for support, had paid for her private school and college tuition, had taken her to father-daughter dances, and occasionally included her in family events with his children by his wife. In addition, Nina was a nationally ranked tennis player, and her father frequently attended her matches, publicly expressing pride in "his daughter." The court accepted her proof of kinship.

Another kinship issue arises when a husband and wife lived separately but never formally divorced. Unless legal steps are taken to disqualify the separated spouse, she has inheritance rights to her husband's estate.

The same goes for a deadbeat parent who abandons a child for most of her life and then shows up when the child dies, hoping to claim a portion of the child's estate.

EXAMPLE: Carla's daughter died at the hands of a reckless driver, and her estate stood to receive a sizeable settlement from the driver's insurance company. When Carla's estranged husband, who had abandoned her and her daughter 12 years ago, heard about the settlement, he showed up hoping to collect half of the money under state intestacy laws. Carla asked the court to disqualify her husband and prevent him from inheriting any of the money.

Less common are distant relatives who claim to be heirs. These heirs must hire a professional genealogist to construct the family tree and submit it to the court to prove kinship and claim their share of inheritance.

THE ESTATE IS NEVER PROBATED

The question of what happens when probate is never filed comes up more often than you'd imagine. Technically, there's no statute of limitations for opening probate, so an estate can remain unprobated for years, even *decades*!

Someone will finally initiate probate when there's a trigger event: someone wants to refinance the mortgage on the family home, or one of the heirs wants to sell or cash out their share.

If years or decades pass, probate can become way more complicated because it may involve multiple estates, multi-generation heirs, and heirs who may not be close or know each other well.

EXAMPLE: Mrs. Torres owned a large home, which over the years had been converted into three separate apartments: her son's family lived in one, her daughter's family in another, and

Mrs. Torres herself in the third. When she died, the children continued to live in the house as before, absorbing the extra space from Mrs. Torres's apartment into the other two. Things worked out fine without probate for decades, until Mrs. Torres's son died, survived by kids and grandkids, and her daughter, now in her seventies, decided she wanted to sell the house and move into a retirement community.

However, since old Mrs. Torres's estate was never probated, the home couldn't be sold because it hadn't been properly retitled after her death. The heirs hired a probate attorney so that the home could be liquidated and the heirs paid out for their share. The attorney had to probate Mrs. Torres's son's estate first, then Mrs. Torres's estate, while dealing with unfamiliar heirs from many generations.

KEY TAKEAWAYS

- Not anyone can contest a will: the contestant must stand to benefit if the will is thrown out.
- There are only three legally recognized reasons to contest a will: it was improperly executed; the deceased was incompetent; or the deceased was under undue influence.
- Minor children can't inherit, so in the absence of a named guardian in the will, the court will appoint one to manage the minor child's money.
- An attorney is almost always needed to probate and settle international estates.
- While there is no statute of limitations on opening probate, estates that aren't probated in a timely manner cause unnecessary expense and delays later on.

NEXT STEPS

You should now feel ready to confidently understand your probate process.

Remember, this guide is not meant to replace the personalized advice of a good probate attorney.

If you need the help of an attorney, you're more than welcome to contact me at <u>probate@anthonyspark.com</u> or 212-401-2990. I'll be happy to get you started.

ABOUT THE AUTHOR

Anthony S. Park is host of the popular podcast *Simple Money Wins* (available on iTunes, Google Play, and anthonyspark.com).

He is a New York executor, attorney, and entrepreneur. Anthony's cases have been featured in many places, including the *Wall Street Journal*, *New York Times*, CNBC, and *MarketWatch*.

INDEX

A
administrator bond, 28–29
assets. *see also* estate, closing process; estate, settlement process
    defined, 34
    determining, 34
    distribution, 59–61
    finding, 36–37
    finding, documents listing, 36–37
    misvalued, 87–89
    non-estate assets, 41–42
    non-probate assets, 34–35
    selling process, 38–40
audits, estate settlement and, 49–50

C
co-executor, 71. *see also* executor(s)
communication, lack of, heirs and, 83–84
community property, 35–36
conflicts, heirs and, 86–95
contested wills, 97–100
    defined, 97–98
    process of, 99–100
    valid reasons, 98–99
cost(s)
    probate process, 15–19
creditors, 43

INDEX

D
debts, estate, 42–43
    versus expenses, 42–43
    paying, 43–44
disabled heirs, 100–101
document(s)
    collection, 26–27

E
estate, closing process, 14, 17–19
    estate account closing, 60–61
    estate accounting, 52–58. *see also* estate accounting
    estate assets distribution, 59–61
    inheritance, 58–59
    overview, 51
    receipt and release, 59
estate, settlement process, 13–14, 17
    assets, determining, 34. *see also* assets
    assets, finding, 36–37
    assets, selling process, 38–40
    audits, 48–50
    collecting, 33–36
    community property, 35–36
    debts *versus* expenses, 42–43
    documents listing, 36–37
    estate account opening, 40–42
    estate *versus* inheritance tax, 46–47
    federal estate taxes, 44–45
    final 1040, 47–448
    non-estate assets, 41–42
    non-probate assets, 34–35
    paying expenses, debts, and heirs, 43–44
    1041 return, 48–49
    state estate tax, 45–46
    taxes, 44–50
    tax returns, filing, 44–50

    value, estimating, 37–38
    will and, 39–40
estate account
    closing, 60–61
    opening, 40–42
estate accounting
    approval by court, 54
    dispute on, 56–58
    lawyer for, 53
    need for, 56–58
    process, 52
    time for, 53–56
estate assets. *see* assets
estate claim, 43
estate(s)
    debts, 42–43
    expenses, 42–43
    international, 101–102
    never probated, 104–105
estate tax, 46–47
    versus inheritance tax, 46–47
executor bond, 28–29
executor(s)
    access to information, 73–74
    complaints about, 92
    complaints from heirs, 72–78
    dual responsibility, 66
    fees, 76–78
    job, challenges, 63–66
    job, managing, 71–72
    job declined by, 69–71
    local co-executor, 67
    long processes, 75–76
    motivation, 94–95
    pay of, 66
    personal risk for, 66
    problem for, 74–75

INDEX

    procrastinated, 92–93
    professional, hiring, 69–71
    right selection, 90–92
    selection, 21, 28, 67–68
    tasks, as non-delegable, 64
    time-bounded operations, 64
    using more than one, 71
    will, role of, 65
expenses, estate, 42–43
    versus debts, 42–43
    paying, 43–44

F
federal estate taxes, 44–45
final 1040, 47–48

H
hearings, kinship, 102–104
heir(s)
    challenges, 81–86
    complaints about executors, 92
    complaints from, 72–78
    conflicts, 86–95
    disabled, 100–101
    executor selection, 90–91
    lack of communication, 83–84
    lack of control, 82–83
    minor, 100–101
    misvalued assets and, 87–89
    money-oriented, 86–87
    overview, 81
    as target, 84–85
    unequal distribution, 89–90

I
inheritance tax, 46–47
    versus estate tax, 46–47
international estates, 101–102
in trust for (ITF) accounts, 9

K
kinship hearings, 102–104

L
lack of communication, heirs and, 83–84
letters, getting, 16
letters testamentary/letters of administration
    described, 25–26
    documents collection, 26–27
    establish eligibility as executor, 28
    getting, 12–13, 16
    overview, 21
    place for probate process initiation, 23–25
    probate bond, 28–29
    receiving, 30–31
    who initiates probate process, 21–22
local co-executor, 67. *see also* executor(s)

M
minor heirs, 100–101
misvalued assets, 87–89
multi-county assets, 23

N
never probated estate, 104–105
non-estate assets, 41–42
non-probate accounts, examples, 9–10
non-probate assets, 34–35

INDEX

O
1041 return, 48–49

P
payable on death (POD) accounts, 9
power of attorney (POA), 10
probate
    contested wills, 97–100
    defined, 5
    fees, 15
    international estates, 101–102
    kinship hearings, 102–104
    minor or disabled heirs, 100–101
    necessity of process, 6–7
    never probated estate, 104–105
    place to process, 23–25
    special situations, 97–105
    stages, 5–6
    time for process, 12–14
    time of process, 7–8
    without a will, 11–12
probate bond, 28–29
probated will
    defined, 6
    need for, 6
probate process
    average time for, 12–14
    cost, 15–19
    estate, closing, 14, 17–19
    estate, settlement, 13–14, 17. *see also* estate, settlement
    initiation, 21–22
    letters testamentary or letters of administration, getting, 12–13. *see also* letters testamentary/letters of administration
    place, 23–25
    who initiates, 21–22
professional executor, hiring, 69–71. *see also* executor(s)

R
receipt and release, estate closing and, 59

S
small-value estates, 10–11
state estate tax, 45–46
summary probate, 10–11

T
target, heir as, 84–85
tax(es)
    estate settlement, 44–50
    federal estate taxes, 44–45
    final 1040, 47–48
    1041 return, 48–49
    state estate tax, 45–46
totten trusts, 9–10
transfer on death (TOD) accounts, 9

V
value
    estate, estimating, 37–38

W
will(s). *see also* probated will
    contested, 97–100
    estate settlement and, 39–40
    improperly executed, 98–99
    probate without, 11–12

Made in United States
North Haven, CT
04 August 2024